MBA INSIDER

How to Make the Most of your MBA Experience

Al Dea

ISBN-13: 978-0-578-61280-5
Library of Congress Control Number: 2019919685

CONTENTS

About the Author

Al is a career and leadership coach, author, and writer. He is also the Founder of *MBASchooled* and *CareerSchooled*, two career blogs that help people build successful careers. His writing and insights have been published in outlets such as *Business Insider*, *The World Economic Forum*, and *Time Magazine*. Al is a Product Marketer at a software company, and previously was a Management Consultant at Deloitte Consulting LLP, where he advised clients on digital transformation and organizational strategy.

Al received his Bachelor's Degree in Business and Theology from Boston College, and his Master's in Business Administration from the University of North Carolina Chapel-Hill. Al is an advocate for economic opportunity for underserved populations, higher education access, talent development, and diversity and inclusion. Al resides in San Francisco, California.

www.**mbaschooled**.com
www.careerschooled.com
Twitter: @Alex_Dea

THE JOURNEY TO BUSINESS SCHOOL

Growing up, the dinner table was treasured in my family. Here, my sister and I would share what we did in school and what was on our minds, and our parents would share what happened at work. Through these exchanges, we learned not only about what our parents did every day but why they made certain decisions that got them to where they were. And so it was, over a plate of broccoli and chicken, where I not only learned about an MBA degree but that I would proclaim at the age of 5, that one day, I would have one too just like my parents.

My Dad is the son of immigrants and Mom came to the United States for her college education and both had earned their MBAs. They frequently talked about how their education had given them opportunities and access to achieving their personal goals and providing the best life possible for my sister and me. Like many young kids, I was influenced by my parents' words, even if I didn't understand them—as evidenced by my decision to tell my family and friends that I would be an engineer, work at Kodak and Xerox, become a firefighter, and get an MBA. Unfortunately, only 20% of those dreams came true.

Even if my dreams were a bit misguided, what I learned was that education was important if I wanted to make a difference and to be successful in life. Internalizing what our parents had taught us, my sister and I both took to school and learning seriously (although her grades were much better than mine). Whether in high school or college, we made a point of making the most of our educational experiences by learning concepts and ideas, pursuing subjects we were curious about, and ultimately learning about ourselves and what we would eventually do in our careers.

After getting a degree in Business and Theology from Boston College, I became a management consultant. Being a consultant is like being a professional learner. You are constantly thrown into situations where you have to get up to speed fast about a new industry, function, or business problem. Since I liked and had gotten good at the practice of learning and learning fast, the role suited me well. While I enjoyed it, after a few years I had a yearning to get back to school. I realized that there were other skills and experiences that I wanted to have. I never felt tied to being a consultant, and I assumed I'd have numerous roles in my career. I also knew that getting back into an academic environment where I'd have time to learn new concepts, be surrounded by smart people, and be in an environment supportive of learning, would help me figure out the other things I might do throughout the course of my career (and maybe I was also trying to make sure I made good on the declaration I made when I was five years old).

Like every other aspiring MBA applicant, I went through the school admissions process, took the GMAT Test, and eventually landed at the University of North Carolina-Chapel Hill. Throughout the process, I gained valuable insights and information about going through the application process, which programs were best for specific industries, and the unique characteristics of the schools. What I was missing was an understanding of what the experience was actually like—the nitty-gritty details of the program, the classes, the highs and the lows, and what students were like outside of brochures, campus tours, and admissions panels.

When I started my MBA, I was inundated with both responsibilities and opportunities. It was a challenge trying to manage all of the priorities and demands of business school.

Whether it was keeping up with my classes, trying to find a new career, or staying in tune with my extracurricular activities, numerous questions would arise, and I constantly sought to make the right decision and choose the right option for whatever was in front of me. I was fortunate to be surrounded by helpful classmates, administrators, as well as MBA alum friends, who offered me advice and guidance to help me throughout the process. However, I certainly had my fair share of stressful moments.

Common Questions about Business School

At the time, as I was one of the first of my friends and professional group to attend business school, I was often asked questions like:

- What was it like to attend business school?
- What did you learn, and what did you do every day?
- How is your experience helping you to grow your career?
- How can I use an MBA to grow my own career?

During my own MBA years, whenever I encountered a new challenge, I reached out to my classmates to understand how they were approaching coursework, navigating the internship recruiting, or figuring out how to select one opportunity over another. Furthermore, I got the chance to meet other students from other MBA programs, and during my conversations, I found that despite going to different programs, we all were asking very similar questions.

To help answer some of these questions I decided to start a blog, *MBASchooled.* This blog was dedicated to answering the questions surrounding what it was like to be a full-time MBA student. Through my blog, research, and further consulting, I heard statements like, “If I had only known then what I know now...” or, “If I had only had a guide with me along the way.”

Over the past five years, I've had hundreds if not thousands of conversations about the MBA experience with current, former, and prospective MBA students. These conversations have covered a variety of topics and questions, but the most common ones I get tend to be the following:

- How will an MBA accelerate my own career aspirations and goals?
- If I get an MBA, how do I go about making the most of the experience, especially considering that I am spending a lot of my time and resources to be there?
- There are so many great experiences and opportunities. How do I know what to select?

This book encapsulates what I've learned, so others can have a guide to navigating the common questions and challenges students encountered throughout their MBA experience. This book covers experiences, insights, and thoughts about key elements of the MBA experience, from the moment students step foot on campus, to recruiting and finding internships, all the way up through graduation and beyond. My hope is that by reading this book you will understand how to navigate business school to build the skills, knowledge, and capabilities to both identify and achieve your current and future career goals.

Who can use this book?

Anyone! But there are two groups of people I had in mind when I was writing this book.

PROSPECTIVE STUDENTS

Treat this like an "insider guide" that gives you behind-the-scenes access to learn about what attending a full-time MBA program could be like. While not all of this will make sense if you are not in school, pay attention to the key moments, mindsets of the students, and key decisions that students make. There is a wide diversity of students and graduates featured in this book; find the ones that speak to you.

CURRENT STUDENTS

Treat this like a playbook, or field guide, that you can turn to throughout your entire MBA experience. During this time, you'll constantly be faced with decisions and opportunities, and at some point, you'll want to find a best practice, contrarian opinion, hot take, or set of recommendations to help you think through a decision or work through a challenge. Use this book to help you move forward.

Note: While this book is geared for those curious about the full-time MBA program, I believe that no matter who you are, a current student or prospective student—or not even a fan of business school, your best path to success starts with you. You have to define your goals as well as develop a path to help you achieve them. However, learning from those who have gone before you or who are experiencing similar things can be extremely valuable. Take the lessons from the students and the insights that are generated as a good starting point, but know that you will need to think this through for yourself.

How to approach reading this book

During business school and my undergraduate studies, I found that I learned best using a combination of learning concepts and practical application through examples, or stories. This model served as a foundation for how I wrote and structured this book. Each chapter is specifically designed to combine all of these elements. In total, there are nine chapters, which span the entire MBA experience, beginning with your acceptance by business school to post-graduation. Each chapter has the following sections:

- **Introduction**: An introduction to the chapter, what it's about, and why it matters. Each chapter was chosen specifically because it highlights a key component of the MBA experience.
- **Spotlights**: Key topics that deserve an extra mention that are often told through the eyes of a former MBA student.
- **Student Stories: Lessons from the Front Line**: First-person stories from MBA students and alums about their experiences and lessons learned for that specific chapter.
- **Key Takeaways**: A summary of the most important lessons from each chapter.
- **Key Questions to Answer**: These are key questions for the topics covered in each chapter. You should reflect upon the chapter and gain insights from these questions.

A foundation for success in an ever-evolving world

The world of work is going through a fundamental transition. In the age of digitization, automation, and acceleration, learning new skills and evolving careers are seen as a regular part of employees' lives. In fact, according to research from *The World Economic Forum*, the half-life of a skill is about five years, which is significantly shorter than ever before. Fortunately, getting an MBA gives you the chance to learn the skills and gain the experiences that are needed to set you up for not just your post-graduation job, but your long-term career. These foundational skills are valuable so that later in your career, you are positioned to find new experiences and opportunities, and that as your company or industry or world evolves, you have the ability to continuously pivot, extend, or grow, too. My goal is that this book shows you how you can navigate your MBA experience to build the skills and gain experiences to consistently set and achieve your career goals, as you continue to progress in life.

As a starry-eyed five-year-old with big dreams, I knew I wanted to get an MBA and go to business school, but obviously, I had no idea why or how it would help me. Fortunately for you, you're smarter than I was because you have this book to figure it out. I hope that it inspires you as you lay out your own career goals and make the most of the opportunities in business school to achieve them.

Happy Reading!

CHAPTER ONE

PREPARING FOR THE MBA EXPERIENCE

Congratulations! You've been accepted to a full-time MBA program. Now the work begins.

Kirsten Smith (UNC Kenan-Flagler, '20) remembers where she was when she found out she got into business school. "I was coming home from work and I immediately rushed home. I jumped for joy, and then went out to celebrate." After the excitement died down, she realized, "Wow, I have a lot of work I need to do before I get to school!"

Preparing for Business School: It's Just Getting Started

MBA candidates spend ample time filling out applications, writing essays, and honing their interview skills to successfully gain admittance to their institution of choice. But it is equally important to prepare for the first year of coursework, which will have a far-reaching impact on job prospects. Getting into an MBA program is tough; studying for the GRE or GMAT, filling out your applications, interviewing with admissions—none of these are small feats. However, while it is a cause for celebration, it is only the beginning of a priority list of actions that lie ahead of you before you even get to school. So, where do you even begin?

Leaving your job gracefully

If you are like most incoming students, you are currently working. One of the first items on the checklist is to break the news to your employer that you're leaving. While some students find this to be easy since their employer is supportive of the decisions and in some cases even involved in the process, for others this is not the case. The best thing to do is to be honest, proactive, and to the best of your ability, lay out a transition plan to ensure minimal disruption. Put together a timeline and have it ready to present to your employer when you have your initial conversation. In addition to business considerations, you'll also need to think about whether you want to take some time off between the end of your job and the beginning of your studies to get your personal affairs in order.

It's very rare in real life to have time for yourself to do nothing, but going to business school gives you an excuse to have time for yourself. Adam Miller (Darden '20) used this to his advantage. Instead of leaving his job right before moving to Charlottesville, VA in July or August, Miller left in March. This allowed him to have time to relax and reflect, which helped him be energized when he got to campus. An obvious thing to take note of and is important to highlight is this: The nice thing about not working is, well, not working. The downside, however, is not getting paid! If you are thinking about this path, make sure to have your finances in order.

Moving to a new city, country, or continent

Ariadne Sabatoski (Fuqua, '20) was excited to move from San Paolo, Brazil to Durham, North Carolina with her husband to attend Fuqua, but she also had so much work to do. "You don't realize how much work is involved, especially when you are moving to a new country."

Leading up to her move, Sabatoski had to do many things to get ready, including filling out the necessary paperwork, finding an apartment and signing a lease, applying for student loans, getting her university transcripts translated, and tracking down her immunization records. She offers the following advice to other students, especially international students: "Take the time to make sure your paperwork is in order. It may seem tedious, but it's necessary."

Even for those who are not moving to a new country or continent, there is still much that has to get done. For Nick Johnson (NYU Stern, '15), the move from Boston to New York City was not nearly as far. Johnson put his consulting skills to use and made a checklist, making sure to complete everything on it. However, by the time he made it to campus, he was exhausted. In the end, it worked out, but he suggests that if you have the luxury of baking in extra time just to get settled, do it. "Being in the right mindset before you enter business school, which will be a stressful and challenging process, is really important. If you can take a few weeks just to get your head in order, I highly recommend it."

Getting into the academic mindset

While moving physically can be challenging and time-consuming, it can also be difficult to shift your mindset from being at work to being back in the classroom. School is different from work as it is a world of classes, lectures, projects, papers, and exams, something that most people don't normally have to deal with in the workplace. Furthermore, for some, especially those who are coming into business school from a non-business background, terminology, language, and general mindset of business school can represent an entirely new way of thinking and working. As a former teacher, Najee Johnson (UNC Kenan-Flagler, '15) was used to the academic environment but did not have a formal business background. Leading up to entering UNC, he made sure to get into the business school frame of mind by reading the Wall Street Journal every day. If you already know what companies you are interested in learning more about, set up Google alerts on them to get up to speed.

Brush up on quant and business topics

Some students come into the program without formal education or experience in quantitative fields, such as finance, accounting, analytics, and economics. If you are among this group (or if you need to brush up), make sure you take the time to learn this material. A growing number of students—even those with a finance background—have come to realize that these additional learning opportunities provide valuable time to network and bond with future classmates before the rush of classes and recruiting hit in the fall.

Reflecting on your aspirations

The MBA admissions process is often a great way for students to reflect upon their career aspirations, but it doesn't need to end there. Shannon Griesser (Fuqua, '19) used this approach leading up to attending Fuqua. Like many other students, Griesser took advantage of the MBA admissions application process to think deeply and reflect upon her past as well as her future aspirations, which ultimately landed her a spot in Fuqua's MBA program. But, as a self-reflective and self-aware person, Griesser took it one step further. "After I was accepted, I made sure to spend time thinking and reflecting on my past experiences and crafting my story and focusing on why I might be a good fit for my desired career path".

Get ready for recruiting

Since the reason for attending business school is to change or accelerate their careers, most MBA students will spend a significant amount of time on career-related activities. Once school begins, MBA students will be inundated with career-related activities, such as resume reviews, cover letter writing, networking emails, mock interviews, and many more fun activities. Since everyone has different comfort levels with these activities, it may make sense to do a little bit of prep work. Sarah Rumbaugh (Darden, '15), the CEO of RelishCareers, encourages students to spend time thinking about their career interests before they come to campus: "The process for internship recruiting starts right away. If you can spend time refining your pitch, updating your resume, and researching a few companies that are interesting, you will put yourself in a great position once recruiting starts."

Pre-MBA internships

Working an internship before business school is another chance to gain experience in and exposure to a field of interest. It can be a valuable opportunity to develop new skills, try a potential new career, or position yourself for summer internship success. While you may or may not have the chance or time to do it, if you are able to it can be a valuable opportunity to develop new skills or try a new career. For example, if you are an operations-focused individual who is trying to break into tech marketing, it might seem like a big leap—but not if you have a few months at a tech start-up under your belt. If this is something you're interested in, make sure to plan ahead.

SPOTLIGHT: Pre-MBA resources & programs

Pre-MBA programs, such as Forté, The Consortium, and Management Leadership For Tomorrow, are all great resources that support students through the MBA admissions and MBA experience. Each program serves a particular mission and a subset of students, but all can be incredibly valuable to students while in business school and beyond.

Forté Foundation

Forté has provided access to education, opportunities, and a supportive network to empower women in business education and management leadership since 2001. Forté is committed to "changing the balance of power in the workplace" and strives to provide women with the resources they need to become leaders in business. The foundation has awarded $180 million in fellowships and has helped nearly 8,000 women pursue and earn an MBA.

Marshelle Slayton (Foster, '19) credits the Forté Fellowship and Forté Foundation not only with helping her to navigate the MBA application process but also with providing her with guidance, support, and resources for her career development. One of the highlights for Slayton was the career development resources provided through Forté. Attending the Forté Conference gave her a chance to build relationships with other fellows, alumni, and leaders. It also gave her opportunities to network and meet with employers in both formal recruiting interviews as well as during informal happy hours. "The resources from the Forté Foundation gave me the chance to hone in on what I wanted and to interview at companies I was interested in even before business school started. Both of these were incredibly helpful to my own development," said Slayton.

The Consortium for Graduate Study in Management

The Consortium is a non-profit organization that helps link students who are under-represented with opportunities to accelerate their development through tuition-based scholarships and support at top MBA programs as well as helping its students find career opportunities with top employers. With over nineteen schools in the Consortium Network, students who apply and are accepted have the chance to gain scholarship money in addition to accessing the career and personal development resources. One of the highlights is the OP, or orientation program, a week-long conference during which Consortium students meet and attend workshops on how to pitch to recruiters, navigate the internship process and interview with recruiters and companies, and potentially lock down summer internship offers even before the school year starts. Jasmine Ako (Yale SOM, '19) found this to be valuable: "The orientation program was a valuable way to prepare for the pace and rigor of MBA recruiting very early. The experience was highly immersive, and it gave me a chance to practice pitching and honing my networking skills before I set foot on campus." Ako also received several internships offers at the OP, which gave her confidence that she could, in fact, use the MBA to pivot careers. She was grateful to the Consortium for providing her with the scholarship and career opportunities, as well as the network of other Consortium Fellows spread across 19 other MBA programs: "transitioning to business school is challenging, but I'm grateful to have a group of people I can always turn to whether it's to study for exams, provide and share career advice, or just hang out."

Management Leadership for Tomorrow

Management Leadership for Tomorrow (MLT) bridges the critical college-to-career transition gap and ensures that our fellows succeed in that "last mile" to post-college careers. By preparing people of color to land and thrive in high-trajectory jobs, MLT delivers immediate and lasting upward socioeconomic mobility. For aspiring MBA students, MLT provides admissions, career, and MBA coaching from expert coaches, alums, and business leaders.

These resources can be significantly helpful in providing MBA students with the insights they need to succeed— far beyond business school. Bryan Smith (Foster, '20) credits MLT with helping him ask important questions, enabling him to redefine his career aspirations. With the support of his career coach, Smith realized that, while he loved sports and the idea of pursuing a career in that field, he didn't actually know why. Working with his Coach through MLT, he recognized some other potential interests that he enjoyed and understood and with the help of the Foster MBA program, he eventually landed an internship at United Airlines.

"I didn't know it at the time," said Smith, "but MLT's questions about what motivates me helped me to clarify my goals and put me on the path for success."

Triston Francis, (HBS, '19) credits MLT for helping him understand the various MBA programs and which ones would best suit his interests. Furthermore, he credits the MLT network as a significant resource throughout his MBA journey. When Francis was interviewing, MLT alums from top consulting firms worked with him on interview preparation and mock interviews to ensure that he was well prepared.

School-Sponsored Pre-MBA Programs

Preparation during the months prior to school can make the transition back into academic life smoother. There are several areas that you can prepare for before your MBA starts.

Some schools have pre-MBA academically minded programs that can help you get acclimated and bring you up to speed on some of the fundamentals of business. In some cases, these are mandatory (if so, you will probably find out in your admissions letter), but for others they are optional. These programs can especially benefit you if you are eager to get exposed to topics like Economics, Accounting, and Finance. They can help ensure that you are ready for the academic rigors of a full-time program. (Note: Many of these have an additional cost on top of tuition.)

Examples of pre-MBA academic programs

YALE UNIVERSITY (SOM)

The Yale University SOM hosts a three-day "math camp" in order to prepare students for the quantitative rigors of an MBA program. Most students who attend these programs come from weaker quantitative backgrounds.

UNC KENAN-FLAGLER

To prepare students for the analytical and quantitative rigors of business school, UNC offers an Analytics Skills Workshop for incoming first-year students. This program takes place over 2–3 weeks in July and offers coursework in Analytical Tools (Statistics), Financial Accounting, and Finance. Besides academic preparation, the program offers career workshops to help students prepare their resumes and build networking and other important communication skills needed to navigate their career search. Finally, it gives students the chance to move in early and start meeting and building relationships with classmates.

MBA orientation

If you have the chance to attend pre-school events, such as orientation, make sure you do so. It's a great chance for you to connect and begin building relationships, which can help you once the year begins. Maureen Keegan (Darden, '17) attended "Darden Before Darden," a 10-day pre-MBA program that prepares students for the MBA experience. It definitely helped ease her transition: "By the time classes started, I already had time to get used to the change in schedule and how busy school was going to be. It was also nice to have a few weeks to get settled in my apartment, especially getting unpacked, before classes started. I also enjoyed getting to meet a smaller subset of my classmates before the entire class showed up."

Social MBA Experiences

Pre-MBA trips

Some MBA programs offer Class Trips that start before the MBA program begins. These are paid trips with your classmates to various parts of the world. Oftentimes, these are great ways to get to know classmates and build relationships before the pressure of the school year begins.

RANDOM WALKS (CHICAGO, BOOTH)

Random Walks was founded in 2001 with the goal of giving Booth students an opportunity to connect with future classmates before they begin their MBA Program. Trips take students around the world and are led by second-year students, allowing you the opportunity to form relationships with classmates before you step foot on campus.

KWEST

The Kellogg Worldwide Exploration Student Trips (KWEST) is a program for incoming first-year students and their partners at Kellogg. Here, second-year students lead groups of first-year students and their partners across the world. By participating in cultural immersion activities, incoming students have a chance to bond and build relationships with each other.

Travel, weekend trips and the cost of travel

One popular element of the MBA experience that is not included in the cost of tuition is travel. While some travel can be for academic classes, much of it exists for social reasons. Trips can be domestic or international and are often planned for large groups of students. For example, many schools will have a student-led ski trip (ex: Utah, Colorado, or British Columbia), but there are also trips that students will plan ad hoc, and those include anything from weekend getaways to Spring Break and anything else in-between. According to *WeTravel*, an online travel platform, on average, MBA students spend $21,296 on travel during the two years of business school.

Travel in business school will vary from student to student. On the one hand, there will be people who travel every weekend and every break, and on the other hand, there will be those that don't.

NETWORKING

Many do it for networking and relationship building purposes. In business, a person's network may lead to important career opportunities, so MBAs are more likely to pay for the opportunity to meet new people.

BUSINESS EXPERIENCE

Many students have a desire to work internationally at some point in their career, and traveling allows them to either learn about a new culture or get experience meeting companies in a specific country that can be relevant down the road.

SEEING THE WORLD

Like any travel experience, seeing a new place or taking in a new culture is a worthwhile experience. Furthermore, there is a time in business school to travel, between holidays and breaks between semesters.

FUN

Sometimes people just want to have fun, especially around others.

Before you get to school, you'll want to spend some time researching the travel opportunities and identifying what you might be interested in. These trips cost money so if you're thinking that travel is going to be important to your experience, you'll want to consider this as you are doing your financial planning for business school. You should consider your own goals for business school, and how travel fits in. There will be lots of opportunities, and while it can be easy to want to take advantage of all of them, making sure you are evaluating how each trip opportunity aligns with your goals can help you decide which ones are right for you.

Since some students come into business school with money or resources, there is a bit of a socioeconomic status that is involved with travel and trips, especially for the more luxurious and opulent experiences. During my time in business school, I mostly traveled for recruiting purposes, taking a few trips to San Francisco to connect with employers and alums. After accepting a full-time offer in the fall of my second year, I decided that I was at a point where I had more time and flexibility and so travel would be more of a priority. In the winter, I studied abroad for a month in South America and used some of the downtimes to explore Chile and Peru with some of my classmates.

During my Spring Break, I visited another friend and classmate who was studying abroad in Italy and a group of us traveled together through Italy and France. For me, my goal for travel was to experience the culture, but also to do so with people that I enjoyed spending time with. How much you decide to travel is up to you, and what you are most comfortable with.

Don't Forget About your Friends and Family

Your time in business school will be focused primarily on you and your own growth and development, so while you have the time, make sure to spend it with the people who matter most, and who you may not get the chance to see or engage with during your time in business school. The MBA experience is going to be a life-changing and exciting one.

STUDENT STORIES: LESSONS FROM THE FRONT LINE

There is so much to get done before the MBA Program starts. Here is how some MBA students prepare for the MBA Experience.

Prepping for your MBA Transition

by Ariadne Sabotski (Fuqua, '20)

Acceptance into Fuqua's MBA Program was a major accomplishment for Ariadne Sabatoski, but it was only the beginning. Over the next few months, Sabotski managed, amidst the chaos of moving and the mountains of paperwork, to prepare to hit the ground running. She shares her story about what it took to ensure that she was set up for success.

After getting accepted to Duke University (Fuqua), I sprang into action to make sure I was ready to attend business school. In addition to physically moving from Sao Paulo, Brazil to Durham, North Carolina, I also had to find the time to prepare for the rigors of an MBA program.

Preparation never stops

Before the application process, I had never seriously considered my long-term goals. The essays pushed me to ask a number of questions: What do I want to do? Where do I want to be? What do I need to get there? After getting accepted, I spent time continuing to prioritize and refine my goals. Recruiting events start right after classes begin, so this helped me stay intentional and take advantage of the resources.

I had two pre-assignments before starting classes. One was an online math review that covered spreadsheets, finance, accounting, statistics, and economics. Only part of the course was required, but I chose to do it all. The second was a training course in Excel software. The five online assignments were due during the first semester, but we were advised to complete as many as possible in advance.

In addition to the main assignments, our Career Management Center had us read a chapter on "Designing Your Life" and adapt our resume to Fuqua standards before orientation.

Managing the paperwork and logistics of a move

One challenge I had was keeping up with the paperwork needed to make the move to Fuqua (apartment lease, student loan, translating school transcripts and immunization records, etc.). It was very time-consuming in addition to packing for the move. If you are an international student, make sure to stay on top of your paperwork!

In the end, I had about five weeks "off" before moving to Durham, and I devoted this time to working on the pre-assignments and traveling to visit family and close friends.

Resources to help along the way

"Fuqua Buddy" is a program that connects first-year students with others who are further along in the program.

My buddy was very supportive, offering advice ranging from where to live to the best supermarket. We also had an International Student Bootcamp to help us adjust to the American education system.

Other resources included access to a Career Fellow (a second-year student who helped with internship recruiting) and a COLE Fellow (another second-year student who helped navigate academic life and the relationship with my first-year team). Both helped keep my decisions aligned with my Professional Development Plan.

Final advice

FINISH YOUR ASSIGNMENTS

Finish your pre-assignments as soon as possible and review your core curriculum so you can take advantage of any exemptions or plan ahead for extra help in a specific course. Looking ahead is the key.

CREATE A PERSONAL DEVELOPMENT PLAN

If possible, I recommend creating a Personal Development Plan before classes start that outlines what you want to take away from business school. Most schools help with this, but having it completed in advance makes you more intentional from the beginning. Write down your priorities and stick to them, but be flexible so you can review and consciously change them if needed.

Prioritizing your MBA Preparation

by Ruchi Singh (Foster, '20)

After deciding to attend Washington University's Foster School of Business, Ruchi Singh focused on the preparation that was most suited to her goals. Ruchi shares her approach to navigating the pre-MBA process and how it helped her transition to Foster.

Focusing on career and recruiting

Before starting class, I wanted to be prepared, and I decided to focus my energy and time where I felt I needed the most help. For example, I spent most of my preparation on career development as opposed to academics. Given my undergraduate major (Economics) and experience in investment banking, I felt comfortable with the academic rigor, and instead, I worked on developing my career search and personal recruiting plan. Coming into business school, I was very focused on recruiting for management consulting, so I researched the recruiting process and implemented the following:

- Read case interview books such as Victor Cheng's *Interview Secrets*
- Prepared my resume and cover letters
- Identified specific experiences and stories I wanted to highlight in future interviews
- Researched companies of interest
- Connected with alumni at companies for coffee chats.

Taking advantage of school resources

Foster has an optional course on professional development that provides guidance on things like updating a LinkedIn profile, career self-assessment, conducting informational interviews, brand essence, resume tips, and an Excel refresher. I was familiar with most of these topics, but the course got me in the right frame of mind.

Since I attended a few pre-MBA events, I needed my resume ready by the end of May. I utilized the Career Management Center's experts for this, which was a huge help, as I received one-on-one attention from them in the summer because they weren't as busy. Furthermore, all first-years had almost a month-long orientation, which included more training in professional development.

Additionally, I did a couple of mock interviews with one of our Career Coaches to practice how to answer key questions I would face in the interview process. My Coaches' feedback helped me hone my interview pitch and stand out in interactions with firms. For case interview preparation, I relied on the Foster Consulting Society (FCS) and second-year students. The FCS had a number of sessions on foundational case prep material that was very helpful, and the students were always available to help me practice and provide feedback on my casing abilities.

Final advice

IDENTIFY PERSONAL STORIES

Before you start, I recommend working on identifying some personal stories you can use in the interview process and polishing your resume before school starts. The fall quarter is extremely busy, so getting this foundational work done during the summer will alleviate some stress.

CONNECT WITH ALUMS

I recommend connecting with younger alumni from your program to ask about industries/career paths you may be interested in. This will help you get a better sense of what you are or aren't interested in.

Making the Most of MBA Prep Resources and Programs

by Julio Santil (Haas, '14)

The MBA application process can be challenging, but there are numerous resources and programs out there. Julio Santil shares his experience with one of these programs, the Consortium, and how it made a difference in preparing for his MBA experience at Berkeley.

How the Consortium helps MBA students

When I first knew I wanted to go to business school, I began talking to my mentors and MBA alums in my network on how I could get guidance and navigate the MBA admissions process. One piece of advice I got was to check out The Consortium. The Consortium is a non-profit organization that connects students who are under-represented with resources like tuition-based scholarships, support at top MBA programs, and career opportunities. There are about 15–20 MBA programs across the United States that have a Consortium presence.

With this knowledge, I applied to the Consortium early in my MBA application process, and while the potential for scholarship money was a major benefit, there were plenty of other resources that I took advantage of prior to stepping foot on campus.

How it works

The Consortium pairs you with current MBA students and Consortium fellows from your school, who are there to answer questions and offer guidance. The Haas Consortium fellows even hosted webinars for us prior to arriving on campus. We also received help in preparing key documents, such as cover letters and resumes. I had spent time on my resume before applying to business school, but I quickly learned that schools have their own desired formats, and mine needed updating.

One of the highlights was the Orientation Program (OP), a week-long event for all the Consortium fellows across all the participating MBA programs. You get a chance to meet the other fellows, attend presentations and lectures, and build your network. The Career Fair at the OP attracts numerous companies that attend for the purpose of interviewing students and making internship offers. A number of my classmates interviewed with companies and received summer internship offers that weekend.

Lifelong relationships

The development resources, lectures, and career and recruiting "prep" are all valuable, but the chance to build relationships with other Consortium fellows was priceless. I have relied on these relationships for advice and guidance for various personal and professional endeavors, and the support and camaraderie are so strong. In my time at Haas, if we needed something, we'd ask the other Consortium fellows, and if we needed a contact at another school, we'd reach out, and someone would be happy to help.

Final advice

USE ALL THE RESOURCES

If you're considering an MBA program, make sure to check out all the programs, organizations, and resources available to MBA students. A friend of mine told me about the Consortium, and I make sure to tell everyone I meet about it as well.

GET INTO "SCHOOL" MODE

I knew that getting back into school mode would take time, so I started reintroducing good academic habits early. Since I knew I was going to be looking for opportunities in the tech industry, I set up email tech alerts, re-read tech blogs daily, and signed up for email newsletters on topics that I thought were relevant.

Taking Advantage of a Pre-MBA Internship

by Nate Jones, (McCombs, '20)

After his acceptance to business school, Nate Jones launched his search for a pre-MBA Internship. Jones shares how his decision to pursue a pre-MBA internship helped him maximize the time before business school.

Finding a pre-MBA internship

Once I found out I was accepted to the University of Texas—Austin (McCombs), I announced the news to my team at the social enterprise I founded and began transition plans. Some of my friends had completed pre-MBA summer internships in industries they wanted to explore which inspired me to consider finding an internship myself. I was interested in a pre-MBA internship for a few reasons:

1. The private equity/venture capital (PE/VC) space is hard to break into and most funds hire people with previous experience.
2. A pre-MBA internship was a low-risk environment—both for myself and for the fund. I could get up to speed and they weren't evaluating me for immediate employment.
3. My main goal for business school was to grasp the private equity investing space and this opportunity was a great way to see the venture capital side.

I emailed an update about my transition to my network and someone suggested I reach out to a few VCs that I thought were interesting. That led me to Kapor Capital.

My path to a pre-MBA internship

I'd previously met people from the Kapor Capital team at a pitch competition, so I contacted them to see if they took summer interns. They pointed me to their application, and after a round of interviews, I landed the summer internship. Most VCs either blog or tweet often and simply engaging with them on their medium of choice is a great way to start the conversation. Make sure to do your homework and wait a few months for the conversation to mature before making a request!

The pre-MBA internship experience

My internship position was as a summer associate on the investing team at Kapor Capital in Oakland. The fund's thesis focuses on closing gaps of opportunity for people of color and low-income populations. My role on the investing team was to vet some of the companies that pitched us, provide due diligence on deals we considered, write investment memos, and interact at the investment committee meetings.

I attended several networking events with other summer associates and VCs and also participated in SMASH (Summer Math and Science Honors Academy), a Kapor program that provides intensive STEM education to high school students.

Final advice

ASSESS YOUR GOALS

I think most people view business school as a time to reflect and think about the direction of their careers. It's certainly a time for reflection, but I found that some of the most successful students have clear direction before classes start. A pre-MBA Internship can help since it offers another data point to figure out if the path you are on is the right fit.

BUDGET YOUR TIME

I was fortunate to have a pre-summer internship, but during orientation, I realized I wasn't really rested. A lot of my classmates took one or two months off before school to travel or refuel. It's a balance.

ASK FOR ADVICE

Ask people who have been where you are what they would have done in retrospect. Share your goals and ask for their advice. Take some time to reflect on what you want out of your experience and communicate your vision with the firm you hope to work for. Companies that host pre-MBAs are invested in you and want to see you do well, so don't be afraid to share your goals.

Key Takeaways

PREPARE AS MUCH AS YOU CAN

There is a lot that needs to get done. Make sure you have enough time from when you leave your job to when school starts to get everything done.

ACADEMIC PREP PROGRAMS

Academic prep programs can make a difference, especially if you are a career switcher or do not have significant exposure to key courses, such as Finance, Accounting, and Analytics.

PRE-MBA INTERNSHIPS

If you want to complete a pre-MBA internship, you'll need to plan in advance. Pre-MBA internships can be valuable, but you'll need to factor in the time it takes to land a role in addition to the duration of the internship.

BE READY TO HIT THE GROUND RUNNING

The experience moves fast, and there is a lot to do. Rest up or take time off to make sure you are refreshed and ready to hit the ground running when you start.

Key Questions to Answer

- What do I need to do in my current job to appropriately tie up loose ends and gracefully exit?
- Who are the people who matter most to me, and how can I spend time with them before business school?
- Do I have the time/interest/resources to take on an MBA internship?

CHAPTER TWO

TRANSITIONING TO MBA LIFE

Times of transition are challenging in all aspects of life, and the transition from work back to school is no different, especially for MBA students in the first semester. This chapter will highlight the transition process students go through and how to best navigate it for success.

After living in the mid-Atlantic region for most of her life, Kirsten Smith (UNC Kenan-Flagler, '20) packed her things and moved to Chapel Hill, leaving her friends and family behind. In addition to moving from work back to the classroom and from Washington, D.C, to North Carolina, Smith was leaving behind a place she knew for an unfamiliar environment. "Moving to school was challenging because it meant developing new routines, building new relationships, learning new academic material, and defining new goals for myself," Smith said. "Fortunately, that also presented lots of opportunities in the first year of business school."

Many students like Smith are moving to a new city, state, or even country, and that is further complicated by the adjustments that must be made any time one moves, whether that's getting used to a new commute, figuring out your childcare options if you're a parent, or just finding the time to take care of normal life's business (e.g., doctor's appointment).

What Makes an MBA Experience Special?

The full-time MBA offers you the opportunity to steep yourself in a unique experience that you're not likely to find during other periods of your life.

Time to invest in yourself

Business School gives you two years to explore and develop and invest in yourself for both the short term and long term. There are not many opportunities like this in life. While you will have responsibilities and there is much to do, you have a lot of control over how you allocate that time, and where you want to invest that time.

Space to reflect

In the working world, life can get so busy that it is hard to pause and reflect. Business school gives you the opportunity to take a step back to understand what you have done and to think deeply about what you'd like to do in the future. It gives you the chance to reflect upon your goals and values, and a chance to build the skills and experiences to achieve those goals.

Resources to make sense of it all

Making time to reflect on your past experiences and future goals is important, but not everyone does this alone. Having experts and thought leaders like professors, professionals, and administrators advising you as you work through your reflection and learning is a critical component to helping you make sense of what you've done and where you want to go. They provide guidance and best practices to help you make sense of how your skills and experiences can lead to a new opportunity, or tactical coaching or insights to make that transition happen.

People who will enrich your life

You are surrounded by a diverse community of talented and driven individuals, whom you can learn from, collaborate and build personal and professional relationships with. This gives you the chance to learn from a diverse group of your peers on topics you previously didn't know about or to share with your classmates experiences such as projects, case competitions, or other initiatives that can help you learn and grow.

A stimulating and supportive environment

While failure isn't "free," it costs a lot less in a learning environment such as business school. Whether that's by taking a class you normally wouldn't have taken because it was on a subject you weren't strong in, taking on a club leadership role, exploring an entrepreneurial idea, or trying a new career or industry, the full-time MBA experience gives you the opportunity to try things, knowing that they may not work out but that it will still be OK. Business school is a safe environment to test out new ideas. If you fail at your first attempt at a project or initiative or career, you would have learned some valuable lessons. And that failure is far, far less consequential than if you do that in a job situation. Furthermore, you are surrounded by many other people who can assist and provide guidance as you navigate and learn from the experience.

The Transition to MBA Life

MBA programs are multi-dimensional experiences. Whether it's in the classroom and getting acclimated to academic courses, spending time in workshops or events to learn about a new career or industry, or taking advantage of the various extracurricular activities, adjusting to the various dimensions of business school life has its own brand of challenges.

Academics

MBA programs structure their calendar in a variety of ways, but most tend to either be on the semester or quarter system. Typically, the first semester (or first two quarters) tends to be the most academically rigorous period of the full-time program. For some of you, the curriculum can be a lot to take in, especially for students who haven't had experience in these subjects. Learning new material about a topic you are familiar with can be challenging in and of itself, but if you don't have any expertise or experience with a course, and in some courses, multiple classes, it can be even more difficult. Furthermore, if you are like many students entering business school, it's been a while since you have been in a classroom, and after a few years of work, you might be a little rusty when it comes to lectures, tests, study groups, and midterms.

Recruiting and career

Students choose to attend business school to accelerate their career growth, and one of the critical elements of that is finding a summer internship. It's key to remember that recruiting starts fast! As soon as you step foot on campus recruiting begins. This means that companies will be on-site right away, second-year students will be sharing their experiences of summer internships, and student clubs will be offering advice and guidance. Be prepared to edit your resume and hone your elevator pitch without delay. As Nick Johnson (NYU Stern, '15) said, "This is the first time many MBA students are asked to think deeply and frequently about their career aspirations for both the short and long term, and that can be both exciting and scary."

Student organizations and clubs

Just as in college, student clubs and organizations bring a vibrancy to student life in MBA programs. They are often the lifeblood of an MBA program. These groups facilitate many opportunities for learning, development, and relationship-building amongst members of the class. There are endless events, lectures, workshops, and social events that can be valuable to developing your network with other students, faculty, and administrators. They give you the chance to take on leadership roles in managing and leading a student club, an organization, or a specific activity. Often, they provide forums where you can enhance your knowledge of a field or function and network with recruiters. Whether it's through planning events where you connect with alums in your field, or working alongside recruiters and hiring managers who are interested in speaking to your student organization, these clubs and organizations set the stage for you to build relationships and learn more about a field or industry.

Social life

A highlight of business school is getting to know your classmates and the greater MBA community, especially through formal and informal social endeavors. There are endless happy hours, networking events, ad hoc or planned socials, and the like. This can be both exciting and overwhelming, particularly when you have other important priorities, such as classes or recruiting, which seem, at least on the surface, more important or of more value. This is something that Smith experienced while at UNC, where she struggled to balance social activities with schoolwork and recruiting: “Building relationships with my new classmates was really important to me, but I had so much going on in those early months. My initial focus was on recruiting and academics, and while I felt guilty saying no to social events, I knew it was the right thing for me, at least early on. Once I felt that I had a handle on my courses and my recruiting process, I became much more involved socially and began to build a broader network across my class.”

Handling Fear of Missing Out (FOMO)

FOMO is not only a real-world thing but also a business school phenomenon. The upside of being surrounded by like-minded people focused on the same thing is that there will be opportunities to do just about anything. Whether it's an impromptu weekend trip with your classmates, attending a recruiting event that everyone else is going to, or signing up for a class that everyone else wants to take, you can easily feel like if you don't say yes, you'll be missing out on a huge reward of the MBA experience. But, at the same time, how can you say yes to everything? When Jeff and Katie Ellington entered Wharton, they had recently gotten married and moved across the country. In addition to adjusting to the rigors of the MBA program, they also knew they wanted to make time for each other. "We had to really prioritize the things that were important to us, which meant that we were very clear on what we wanted to say yes to," said Katie. "While it wasn't always easy, we both felt that our choices reflected our priorities of each other, our family, and our interests," added Jeff.

SPOTLIGHT: Adjusting to a move to the United States

Transitions can be challenging for anyone, but especially for those who are moving to a new country and learning an entirely new culture on top of making the move to a full-time MBA program. Each year many international students do this when they come to full-time MBA programs. Reinaldo Caravellas (UNC Kenan-Flagler, '19) made the transition from Brazil to Chapel Hill, North Carolina, and was able to navigate the transition by focusing on key issues.

Start with the basics

Before you even jump into school, start with the basics such as getting groceries, figuring out transportation, enrolling in your new healthcare system, acquiring credit cards, and all the other logistical necessities of daily life. If you are an international student, Caravellas encourages you to research and learn about as many of these as possible prior to moving to the United States. He also acknowledges, however, that some of these matters will have to be addressed after you've physically made the move.

Understand the cultural differences

Depending on where you come from, cultural difference manifests itself in a number of different ways. For Caravellas, the American style of communication was much more direct than what he was used to. "Communicating directly and bluntly was something that was new for me, and took time to adjust to. But working alongside and practicing with my U.S. born classmates helped me get more comfortable with the process."

Ask for candid feedback

Even though there are adjustments that need to happen, there are plenty of students who understand the culture and who can provide context and insight on things that are new or don't make sense. "Ask your American classmates about anything that doesn't make sense, or for honest or direct feedback. They can help you understand why certain things are the way they are, while also highlighting to you what you can improve," Caravellas said.

Your New Classmates

One of the key components of the MBA experience is being surrounded by a talented and diverse cohort of peers. When you enter a full-time MBA program, the number of students will range from 100 to 900, and it's very likely that you're going to be spending every day with these people.

At UNC Kenan-Flagler, Smith was surrounded by 280 classmates each and every day. This is a great opportunity, but it can also be overwhelming to spend 12–14 hours a day with strangers in a brand-new environment. Whether it's in class, at a recruiting event with lots of people, or in a small five- or six-person study team, you are always surrounded by people. This can be both exciting and draining. According to Smith, "As someone who straddles the line between an introvert and an extrovert, this was both fulfilling and draining, depending on the day. I loved learning from my peers and hearing about their experiences, but I also needed alone time to refocus and recharge."

Classes, recruiting events, and formal social events hosted by the school are all great opportunities to get to know your classmates. Some of the best relationships are built through informal and proactive initiatives. For example, at Harvard Business School, Triston Francis (HBS, '19) hosted a series of small group dinners at his apartment on campus. To start each dinner, Triston and his roommate would read the personal statement they wrote to gain admittance to HBS as a way of breaking the ice and diving beyond surface-level conversations. Each student had the chance to share their stories or ask questions, but it was meant to help people get to know each other. "I was pleasantly surprised that my classmates were not only receptive to this idea but genuinely excited to have this opportunity to speak with their peers candidly about deeply personal topics," said Francis.

I feel like an imposter!

The beauty of having a lot of dynamic classmates is that you have plenty of people to learn from during your time in business school. However, it can be easy to feel overwhelmed or to get the "imposter syndrome" because you feel like you don't measure up. Additionally, some schools have highly competitive environments. In many cases, you are competing against your fellow classmates for the same leadership opportunities, internships, or full-time jobs—and this is true even in less competitive schools. This can breed all sorts of insecurities as well as imposter syndrome, especially early on. For example, I struggled with imposter syndrome and with feeling like a fraud as I was making my transition to business school. I was one of the younger students in my class with less experience than most, which made me nervous about whether I could contribute equally. I figured out I had one of the lowest GMAT scores in my entire class, which again made me feel like I wouldn't be able to contribute and that I got lucky just to get in.

All these thoughts were swirling around my head as I stepped onto Chapel Hill's campus. Over time, I came to realize that I was not the only one who didn't totally feel like they belonged there. Many of my classmates had the same feeling for a multitude of different reasons. It took an adjustment of my mindset and my attitude, but over time those fears subsided, and I began to embrace the opportunity to learn things in areas that I wasn't strong in and contribute to discussions, projects, and opportunities where I had experience or talents that I could share. In reality, these are the communities in which you will learn and grow the most, and will offer the best career opportunities, too. Learning to be comfortable in that environment is a valuable life skill. You will have moments when you feel insecure or overmatched. Over time, you'll come to learn from them to become stronger.

Start with your strengths

One of the ways to overcome this is to understand that everyone brings skills and experiences that add value to the program. So even if you feel that you are lacking in one area, you have plenty to offer in others. After spending eight years as a Marine Corps Officer, Richard Porter (UNC Kenan-Flagler, '17) went to business school to transition to a civilian career. Porter's past experience leading teams and working towards goals allowed him to use his leadership skills to lead group projects and student initiatives within the MBA Student Association. "Using my strong sense of mission and purpose along with my skills in driving towards a goal, I was able to use these skills to make a positive impact," Porter said.

SPOTLIGHT: Challenging and difficult moments of business school, and what people learn from them

It's easy to read the brochures and websites and to think that business school is all rainbows and butterflies, but like anything meaningful in life, there are real challenges and difficult moments.

Moment 1: Transition in the first semester

There are many difficult moments, especially during the transition. For example, Jasmine Ako (Yale SOM, '19) felt that the transition to business school during her first semester was particularly overwhelming. "At that time, I hadn't yet figured out how to prioritize between recruiting, academics, extracurricular activities, and my personal life." As a result, she felt she sacrificed her own well-being, and often felt mentally and physically exhausted." To overcome this, Ako began setting clear boundaries for how long she would dedicate to specific priorities. For example, she would put a time constraint (ex: 2 hours) spent on a specific assignment and also making time for moments and experiences that gave her energy. "I genuinely enjoy one-on-one conversations, and meals with others, so I made sure to incorporate those into my schedule amidst all the other activities. These were moments that gave me energy and excitement, and made me feel better, even during hectic or stressful times," Ako said.

Moment 2: Finals week at the end of first semester

For Kellie Braam, (Booth, '18) her most difficult moment was during finals week of her first year. "During finals week, I was stressed about classes and finals, I felt like I wasn't making friends, and was exhausted from two months of corporate conversations." But, it was also at this time that Braam was able to find comfort, as she began to realize that she wasn't the only one. "During that process, I learned that I wasn't alone in feeling like I didn't have everything together. Furthermore, I also learned to keep putting myself out there. I signed up for clubs, and participated in school activities even if I wasn't entirely sure what they would entail. Sure enough, and over time, I built strong bonds with some of my classmates."

Moment 3: Facing rejections from companies during internship recruiting

It's very rare for any student to knock every interview out of the park, and with that comes rejection, which can be difficult to overcome. During his internship interviewing process, Griesser was rejected by a number of different companies, and during some of those moments, she began to question her own abilities. "When you see your friends getting the jobs that you aren't, you begin to question what's wrong with you?" During those times, it can be easy, and dangerous, to let those decisions define you, but instead, Griesser took those moments to evaluate the feedback, and learn from those opportunities to move forward. "What helped was having a supportive group of peers, administrators, and professors, who could both empathize with you because they have been in your shoes, and provide honest counsel and feedback to help you improve. It is not always fun, but having the confidence to keep moving forward, and using the great support system around you help you overcome difficult moments."

Moment 4: Graduating without a job

During his last week of business school, Jason Perocho (UNC Kenan-Flagler, '15) went through his own challenging moment, when he realized that while many of his peers had jobs, he did not. "I looked up, realized that everyone had a job, and felt like while I loved my time in business school, that I had done it all wrong." For Perocho, that feeling of "being behind" or not on par with his peers gave him concerns, but upon reaching out to other mentors and alums, he realized he was exactly where he was supposed to be. Since he was interested in full-time opportunities at technology companies who primarily focus on "just-in-time" recruiting, securing a job only a few weeks in advance of starting is not uncommon.

With this realization, Perocho focused his efforts on finding a full-time opportunity. Sure enough, within a few weeks, he landed a job. "It can be easy to feel behind and begin questioning yourself when everyone else is doing something different, but it's important to remember that if you want to achieve your own goals, you have to focus on what you can do to achieve your own goals, and not worrying about others," Perocho added.

Transitions are Challenging, and that's Okay!

The MBA program is a rigorous and time-consuming experience. In particular, the first semester (or first two quarters) is a huge change for many people. With all these big adjustments (and there are others), students are often overwhelmed on the first day and drinking from a firehose. They are meeting new people, being exposed to numerous companies, and juggling multiple competing priorities all while trying to maintain some sense of balance. It's an arduous and rigorous task. Many people feel overmatched, overwhelmed, and underprepared. So, what's the good news? Each year, thousands of MBA students make it through their first year of business school, eventually graduate, and go on to enjoy successful careers. That means you will too.

Student Stories: Lessons From The Front Line

Transitions in life can be difficult, but they are also periods of learning and growth. The following MBA students have successfully navigated their own transitions to business school and provide some tips and best practices for current and future MBA students.

Building and Maintaining Relationships in Business School
by Katie Blach Ellington (Wharton, '17)

Throughout her life, relationships have been important to Katie Blach Ellington. As such, moving from the Bay Area to Philadelphia to attend Wharton was certainly a challenge and opportunity. Despite the hectic schedules and time constraints of business school, Blach Ellington traveled the world and played club hockey, while continuing to juggle the many important relationships in her life, such as one with her classmate (and husband) Jeff.

Fighting the MBA stereotypes

Whenever I have conversations about business school, I find that common stereotypes rear their heads. For example, many people talk about business school as being nothing but a two-year party…, globetrotting, and lots of parties. While there are a lot of fun experiences, classes are challenging and recruiting and extracurricular activities can be huge time commitments. While people like to talk about the fun experiences, everyone I encountered in my time at Wharton had real goals around personal development, career transition, and augmented skill sets.

Overcoming challenges

Business school throws you all sorts of different challenges. For me, one challenge was transitioning back to being a student. While the student schedule allows a lot more flexibility than a work schedule, there's always something hanging over your head. It took me a while to get back into the student mentality. Another major challenge for me has been balancing my previous relationships with my new life within the Wharton community.

My husband was also a first-year student at Wharton, and I at times found it difficult to schedule quality time together given the enormous amount of social and extracurricular activities here. By the time you're in business school, you also have friends from many different life stages as well as your family. Early on during my experience, it was difficult for us to manage time between our loved ones and our new friends within the Wharton community. It can be easy to get completely immersed in your business school community, but make sure to take the time to nurture the relationships that you care about!

Building great memories and relationships

One of the most memorable experiences I have from my first year at Wharton was playing ice hockey. I had only ice skated a few times as a kid, but I'm a huge San Jose Sharks and Boston College Eagles hockey fan, and when I heard that playing co-ed ice hockey was a big thing at Wharton, I was all in. It was an incredibly fun and humbling experience. My team also has an amazing camaraderie; it was great to meet people when you're all out of your comfort zone because it puts everyone on the same level.

Final advice

REMEMBER YOU HAD A LIFE BEFORE BUSINESS SCHOOL

In my case, I had a very real reminder because my husband was in school with me! But make sure not to forget about the relationships and things in your life you had prior to entering school. Yes, it will change, and you won't devote the same amount of time to them now that you have school, but if they are a priority you should not feel guilty making time for them.

TAKE ADVANTAGE OF BEING IN ACADEMIA

One of the benefits of being in an academic setting is the access to the professors and learning, it's hard to get these elsewhere. I loved taking advantage of all the amazing speakers, workshops, field trips, and just learning. This is hard to replicate in the real world.

TRAVEL

The other two best experiences from my first year have been the Wharton Global Immersion Program trip I did in Southeast Asia over winter break, and the Wharton Japan Club Trek I did over spring break. While I know the international trips can be difficult to swallow because of the cost, do them. It will stretch your comfort zone, expose you to new cultures, and also strengthen relationships with your peers. Travel is an amazing way to build relationships.

Navigating the Chaos of the MBA Transition

by Ben Thayer (UNC Kenan-Flagler, '16)

After starting his career as an engineer, Ben Thayer came to business school to find a new career, and jumped into his classes and recruiting. He shares some of the challenges he encountered and how he was able to overcome them.

Let me say it bluntly: The first semester of business school is nuts. It's crazy. Every day brought new rewards that reminded me that I made the right decision to quit my job. However, at least once a week, I'd wake up and wonder how I was going to survive. I went to college with the intention of being an engineer for the rest of my life, so I had little education or experience in business. But, I realized that people get MBAs for all sorts of reasons and from all sorts of backgrounds. Whenever I had a moment of doubt, I leaned on my first- and second-year classmates, who provided guidance and counsel that helped me feel confident about my decision.

Fighting imposter syndrome

Business school is funny because while everyone is very intelligent and hard-working, many of us were stressed out about our faults. It was easy to feel the imposter syndrome among so many smart people. But, if you look within, you realize everyone has something to offer. Everyone has his or her own unique strengths and experiences as well as their weaknesses, and putting these strengths to work can add real value. This all came to action when we were preparing for our Economics exam. In the study session leading up to it, our Professor mentioned a specific problem about which nobody had any idea what he was talking about. However, we sprang into action and divided up re-reading notes, reviewing videos and searching through the textbook. Sure enough, it was on the exam, and because we were prepared, we earned high marks.

UNC Kenan-Flagler divides each semester into two "mods." Mod 1 was easier for me, as the analytical bent of the coursework matched up well with my engineering background. Mod 2 was much more challenging really and I had to push myself to speak up in non-linear case discussions and learn how to pick apart different business strategies. This was both gratifying and humbling, in that you could feel great after one class where the material clicked, and feel completely helpless in another when it didn't make sense. Learning to appreciate both of those experiences was humbling but having classmates to support you through both types of experiences was gratifying.

Final advice

ASK FOR HELP

At times I felt out of place, especially during the early stages due to the transition I was making. The good news is that there are literally hundreds of students who have done this before. The second-years were so helpful in providing guidance, assistance, and feedback to small and big questions I had. You don't need to do this alone.

KNOW YOUR PRIORITIES BUT TAKE THE LONG VIEW

With activities, academics, recruiting, and social life, it can be easy to feel overwhelmed. Spend time on each, but take the long view. It's okay to turn in a sub-par case write-up if you were at a recruiting dinner the night before, but make sure your next case for that professor is high quality. I was tempted to focus exclusively on my classes and clubs, but it was nice to give myself some flexibility and grab some drinks on a Tuesday. Who knows, the guy or girl next to you at the bar might help you get your internship (Note: this actually happened to me!)

SET GOALS AND REMIND YOURSELF OFTEN WHY YOU'RE IN BUSINESS SCHOOL

Take risks and push yourself. You want to leave school knowing that you gave it everything you had because you'll never have this chance again. Also, this is the safest environment to take a risk, surrounded by so many peers and resources.

Building and Balancing Relationships and Life in Business School

by Kirsten Smith (UNC Kenan-Flagler, '20)

After living in the mid-Atlantic region for the majority of her life, Kirsten Smith relocated to Chapel Hill to attend UNC Kenan-Flagler, moving away from a strong network of friends and family. During her first year, one of the biggest adjustments she had to make was getting acclimated to her new lifestyle, which meant making new friends, finding new routines, and balancing a busy schedule.

Adjusting to a new environment

I was surprised to find that for me the biggest adjustment was relocating and rebuilding my social life. I lived in the same 1.5-hour bubble for my entire adult life between Baltimore, Pennsylvania, and D.C. Coming to business school in Chapel Hill, I left all that behind. For the first time, I really felt alone. I no longer had my network of friends or my safety net of family, and I hadn't realized how physically and emotionally isolating that would feel.

Furthermore, coming into school, I naively assumed that because I would be surrounded by 280 people making friends would come easy, but it took time and effort. I looked for various opportunities to build relationships with my peers. At UNC, we are split into "Legacies" of about 35 students, who all take classes together in the first and second modules. This allowed me to get to know my classmates in a much smaller setting. I also took advantage of our Legacy Cup events, such as trivia, karaoke, and bowling, because I wanted to form close relationships with the people that I was taking classes with every single day.

Managing your B-school social life

While I very much enjoyed getting to know and building relationships with my classmates, I'm one of those people that falls just over the line toward being an introvert. I really enjoy socializing, but I do need my alone time to regroup. If you're like that, then you simply have to accept that that's how you operate best, and it's okay to not be at every single event. Otherwise, you will find yourself completely exhausted or experiencing FOMO all the time!!

I found that in Mods 1 & 2 (the first two quarters) it was difficult to make time for social events due to conflicts with review sessions, company presentations, club events, lectures, etc. But, once the academic and recruiting schedules lightened up in Mod 3, I began to prioritize social activities more. I also tried to make time for informal or ad hoc events, whether that was hosting a dinner party or going out for drinks with friends.

Despite how busy it is in the first year—and especially the first semester—of business school, it's still extremely important to make time for your personal life. As you start to become overwhelmed by the intense coursework, the rigor of recruiting, and the challenge of building a social life, remember that you had a life before business school. Don't neglect relationships with friends and family; they're lifelines during times of stress. I am also in a long-distance relationship, so it was a major priority for me to make time to see my boyfriend back in D.C. In addition, for your own sanity be sure to exercise. It's a helpful way to take an hour or so for yourself and de-stress in a healthy way.

Final advice

GIVE IT TIME

Despite what you may think and despite how it may happen for some, making friends does not necessarily happen overnight or even within the first few months. I strongly recommend getting involved early as a way to get to know a wide variety of people. I found case competitions to be a great way of accomplishing this because you form small teams with people to focus on a unique challenge for a short period of time, which forces you to get to know each other quickly.

PARTICIPATE IN GROUP ACTIVITIES

Even as an introvert, I appreciate group activities. These are great ways to build relationships. For example, my closest friends came from participating in case competitions and in student organizations. Going into my second year, five of my closest friends will be serving on club leadership boards alongside me. As you start to meet more people, you'll naturally gravitate toward some more than others.

SAY YES

Once you do find "your people," say "yes" to as many activities with these people as possible, everything from a quick and casual bite to eat, to a movie or game night, to a night out. The more that you show that you're willing to participate and engage, the more that socializing will become natural. Also, it's completely normal to find two or three people that you genuinely feel closest to within a larger group of friends. Just remember that not all 280 classmates will be your best friends—and that's okay.

Accelerating the Transition by Immersing yourself in the United States Culture

by Nishanth Kadiyala, (UNC Kenan-Flagler '16)

After growing up, going to college, and working in India, Nishanth Kadiyala moved to Chapel Hill, North Carolina to attend business school. During his research, he learned from others about the importance of navigating the transition to the United States and made sure to take advantage of all the resources at UNC to ease the transition.

From my conversations with international students and alumni I knew that adapting to the culture was one of the first things I needed to do when I got to campus. I jumped in headfirst to learn about the American culture. Whether it was sports, literature, history, or traditions, I tried to absorb as much as I could. Fortunately, many of my classmates were more than happy to help. I invested my time in improving my personal brand. International students are usually stereotyped as someone with limited communication skills and leadership abilities—and sometimes justifiably so. To transform myself into an eloquent leader, I joined public speaking classes in preparation for school. I took advantage of the Business Communication Center to practice and perfect my elevator pitch, and having conversations with recruiters and employers. I also actively sought feedback from my American counterparts and professors to consistently get better at presenting myself.

USING THE SCHOOL'S RESOURCES TO ACCLIMATE PROPERLY

UNC has dealt with several generations of international students which made it easy for the school to acknowledge the culture gap and find ways to encourage students to bridge that gap. The school ensured that the sections and study groups were culturally diverse. There were a lot of clubs that allowed students to find common interests and hobbies that transcended national boundaries. When it came to celebrating festivals, we celebrated the world. Americans invited us to Thanksgiving dinners, Indians celebrated Diwali, Brazilians hosted soccer parties, the Japanese shared their traditions, etc. The success of all of this comes down to the culture of the school. UNC ensures that they are consistently finding the right group of people to keep the UNC culture intact. Finally, one of my favorite resources was Professor Tim Flood's orientation class for International Students. This class took on some of the most common challenging elements of business school for International students and addressed them in an open, blunt, but honest way. It created a safe space for international students and Americans to discuss topics like how to greet each other, how to share feedback without offending one another and how to accommodate introverted and extroverted cultures. All these and more were covered early on and kept all of us in a growth mindset.

Final advice

BE CURIOUS

I recommend that international students be genuinely excited, curious and passionate about learning from the US culture. If you see the cultural gap just as a requirement or a roadblock, then that is what it becomes. But, if you see that as a good opportunity to learn about the lives, personalities, culture, and history of a similar yet different kind of people, then you will very much enjoy these cultural shifts.

TEACH OTHERS

While you learn to fit into the American culture, it is important to teach your American friends how to accommodate you as well. As MBA grads aspire to be globally relevant, it is equally important for the American counterparts to learn about your culture too. So, this cultural shift doesn't have to be a one-way street. All of us can be both a student and a teacher.

Key Takeaways

The transition to MBA life requires major adjustments, but it also presents opportunities to take advantage of. Remember these key points:

PRIORITIZATION BECOMES CRITICAL

Business school is a huge exercise in prioritization. Whether it's across social or academic life, recruiting, or clubs, figuring out what to say yes or no to is critical to adjusting to the new pace.

THE VALUE OF YOUR CLASSMATES AND SECTIONS

Getting to know and learn from your classmates is a key value of the MBA program. It can be overwhelming to be surrounded by so many people for so many hours of the day, but take advantage of this opportunity.

FOMO IS REAL

It can be easy to get caught up in saying yes to something because you are afraid of missing out if you say no, but it is a relief when you learn to say no to things that truly are not aligned with your priorities.

MAKE TIME FOR YOURSELF

We're all human, and we need time to unwind, relax, and recharge. Be sure to always give priority to your own health and well-being.

FIGHT IMPOSTOR SYNDROME

Even among smart and intelligent classmates, remember that you belong and have unique talents to contribute to others, and there will be many great opportunities to learn from others as well.

Key Questions to Answer

- How do I want to prioritize academics, career development, extracurricular activities, social life, and personal time?
- For everything I'm doing this semester, what are the things I have done before versus the things I haven't?
- What are the best ways for me to connect with my classmates to build relationships?

CHAPTER THREE

THE MBA ACADEMIC EXPERIENCE

Moving back into the classroom after years in the professional workplace is exciting but can be intimidating. The MBA academic experience provides countless opportunities to learn, grow, and expand your knowledge—you just need to know how to take advantage of them.

Alexandra Jaeggi (Marshall, '20) entered business school with a desire to transition from a career in teaching to one in marketing in the technology industry. As a self-proclaimed "poet," Jaeggi was excited to learn more quantitative skills, and for the opportunity to be challenged in the classroom. Despite worry about her lack of experience with topics such as finance and accounting, Jaeggi was able to achieve her goals, especially through utilizing the learning resources that her school provided. "With great resources, such as extra study sessions, strong Teacher Assistants (TAs), and accessible professors, I was able to master topics that I didn't previously have exposure to," Jaeggi said. "The MBA course load can be daunting, especially for areas where you don't have expertise or experience, but like I used to tell my students, you have to use all your resources."

MBA Academics

While your skills and business insight might be honed by years in the trenches, learning in the academic environment can present unique challenges such as new material being thrown at you in a short amount of time. The

MBA academic experience requires a serious commitment of time and effort and in the following chapter, we will discuss topics such as the academic structure, core and elective classes, and strategies for how to learn best.

Structure

Every program structures its classroom experience and overall course schedule in a unique way. Below are some examples of how different programs structure the academic calendar:

DUKE UNIVERSITY (FUQUA)

The academic year is organized into four six-week terms of MBA classes that each meet twice a week for two hours and 15 minutes. Classes meet Monday–Friday, with the exception of Wednesday, when classes do not meet.

UNC KENAN-FLAGLER

The academic year is organized into four "Modules" starting in August and ending in May. In each Module, students take an average of five courses. Course length is generally either 50 minutes three times a week (Monday, Wednesday and Friday) or one hour and 15 minutes twice a week (Tuesday and Thursday).

Core classes

All students in MBA programs start off their first term with what is known as the "core." This is a set of business basics and fundamentals, such as Finance, Marketing, Operations, Strategy, Data & Analytics, and Organizational Behavior. With the "core," you get an introduction to the key aspects of business, and a chance to explore a variety of different functional areas.

Since students come from diverse backgrounds, they have varying degrees of familiarity with these topics.

Someone who has been an investment banker probably will be very comfortable in the Finance class, whereas the marketers will breeze through Marketing 101. Regardless of your experience, there are some nuances that make even a familiar topic difficult. First, you are taking many of these classes all at the same time. This can be particularly overwhelming for students who don't have a formal business background. It is a lot of information to digest and understand in a compressed time frame. Second, even for those who studied the subject before, there is still a ton of material to learn and at a depth that is far greater than that of the undergraduate level. Finally, core classes are often taught at the same time to help you understand that while the functions or disciplines are separate, they are actually integrated. Just as a financial decision can have implications for the marketing department, so what you learn in finance can be integrated with what you learn within marketing.

The good news is that you will not be alone. All students take the same classes at the same time, so you'll be in good company as you navigate through those first few months of school.

Elective classes

While most of the first part of your first year will be devoted to core classes, you will have the ability to start taking electives usually in the second half of the first year and then for all of the second year. Elective courses give you the chance to learn deeper into a chosen field of specialization and round out your general business acumen with more specialized insights, most likely pertaining to either your post-MBA career or an area of interest.

Electives gave Najee Johnson (UNC Kenan-Flager, '15) a chance to pursue his post-MBA interests along with topics he was curious about or interested in. With a desire to transition into management consulting, Johnson made sure to take some analytical and general management classes, but he also left room for courses he knew he'd be engaged in because he simply enjoyed learning about the topic. As a career switcher, Iman Nanji, (Anderson, '20) used her elective courses to round out important subject areas where she had less comfort and experience. This helped her prepare for her summer internship and to take on a new field.

SPOTLIGHT: How to pick your electives

As a first-year MBA student at UNC Kenan-Flagler, Kirsten Smith (UNC Kenan-Flagler, '20) wanted to pursue a concentration in Marketing and Data Analytics. To do this she developed the following approach, which tailored her electives to meet her academic and career interests.

Review concentration guides

Schools have concentrations or specific areas of study. Kirsten reviewed the guides and figured out which electives were aligned to the areas she was interested in.

Talk to second-years

Afterwards, Smith connected over coffee with some second years to get their perspective. If she heard repeatedly that a professor was great but it wasn't a class that she had been considering, she usually put it on her list.

Select ones of interest

While Smith tried to align most of her courses to her field of study, she also took classes that looked interesting, even if they weren't directly related. She considered this her final academic experience and wanted to make it count.

Building a well-rounded business foundation

Part of the value of an MBA is that it gives you a cross-functional disciplinary perspective to enable your success in whatever career comes next. So, while it makes sense to focus your electives on your interests, or immediate career aspirations, it's also important to develop a well-rounded business toolkit. To do this, identify what you need to learn and what you want to learn based on your career aspirations and interests. Look for opportunities to strengthen your knowledge in areas that complement your strengths. If you are more quantitative-based and love financial modeling, make sure to take a few other classes to complement your quantitative background. Likewise, if you want to build a career in marketing, consider taking an accounting or finance elective, as one day you might be asked to manage your team's budget. It's impossible to cover all subjects, but having enough self-awareness to complement your key strengths or core areas with some additional diverse skills or classes will give you enough exposure to other areas of business that can be helpful to your future career.

The Classroom Experience

Similar to undergraduate learning, there are lectures in which professors cover specific topics. Generally, there is a reading, or case, or an assignment of sorts, and the class covers them together. Class participation is generally encouraged and is one of the highlights of the experience. The MBA program is a unique graduate program because the majority of students have prior work experience. In fact, the experiences that students bring into the classroom is often a highlight of the MBA Program. That indeed was the case for Charlie Mangiardi (NYU Stern, '17). Previously, he had worked in the non-profit sector and had minimal exposure to topics like accounting and finance, but learning about his classmates' experiences in these areas helped him grasp the ial in a much more tangible way: "There's nothing more fascinating than sitting in a strategy class and having class discussions with consultants, aspiring doctors, and an untold number of other experts. It makes you think through business challenges in a way that you just cannot be exposed to without coming to a place like this."

SPOTLIGHT: From the military to business school

Prior to attending London Business School, Andi Frkovich (LBS, '20) was a Surface Warfare Officer in the U.S. Navy. Like many other students, she faced her own unique challenges with adjusting to a new environment, and for her, it revolved around her initial lack of business knowledge. To overcome this, she took advantage of as many resources that her program had to offer, such as office hours with professors, and learning from classmates who had extensive expertise in a particular topic. She also made a commitment to read the Financial Times and other business media publications every day. "Through dedicated habits, I gradually became more comfortable with the terminology and topics," Frkovich said. She also found other areas where she could contribute right away. "My leadership skills that I built in the Navy were valuable in working on teams, helping set a goal, and working to execute against it," Frkovich said.

Grades

Some schools have traditional grading policies (A, A-, B, etc.) while others use a modified policy (high pass, pass, fail, etc.). Some do not use grades at all. Furthermore, some schools do not disclose grades to employers while others do. The grading policies tend to correlate to the rankings of the schools (e.g., top-ranked schools tend to have grade non-disclosure policies).

This matters for a number of reasons. If you do have a grading policy at your school, this will certainly play into your study team dynamics. If you have five people on a team but some people want to get an A while others are content with a B-, how do you manage workload and output for everyone? Additionally, as you individually manage your own workload and priorities, you'll need to consider how much effort you want to put into specific classes to ensure you get the grade you want. While it's laudable to get an A in every class, given all of the other priorities you have, such as recruiting, you need to decide if spending all that time studying is the best use of your resources when you have other goals to achieve. And finally, for certain industries, grades in specific classes can sometimes be important. For example, if you are a career switcher going into investment banking, it makes sense to make sure you get a good grade in your Accounting and Finance classes. So, do grades matter? The answer is it depends. While getting a top grade is never a bad thing, some argue that it might not be reasonable to expect to get a top mark in every single class. However, that doesn't mean you shouldn't try. Nick Johnson (NYU Stern, '15) said, "I wanted to be pushed in business school, so I put forth my best effort in specific classes where I wanted to drive my learning. However, operating at that pace was not sustainable for every single class, which meant I had to prioritize." Every student is different, but this is a judgment call you will have to make based on what makes sense for you personally.

Pushing yourself to think bigger than just grades

One of the advantages of business school is that it affords you the chance to explore classes that interest you, even if you don't have enough experience to feel comfortable with the topic. There were a number of such classes that I took in school that fell into this category. I was optimizing for learning, knowing that I would not necessarily get the same grade as I would have on a more familiar subject. While nobody wants to get low grades, it's also important to acknowledge the value that comes from learning when you aren't solely focused on the letter grade at the end of the course. During her time at Fuqua, there were classes that Shannon Griesser (Fuqua, '19) was interested in that were challenging. While she knew she wouldn't fail the classes, she also realized she probably wasn't going to get the highest grade: "I wanted to push myself to learn, and needed exposure and practice. It was less about getting the perfect score, and more focused on learning the material."

Learning Teams: Teamwork Makes the Dream Work

One hallmark of the MBA experience is the amount of team-based work that occurs, especially within the classroom. While team-based assignments are not foreign concepts to those who had them in undergraduate studies, they make up a significant portion of the MBA classroom experience. At most schools, students are assigned to learning teams when they enter the program. These teams consist of four to six students. They are usually made up of students with whom you take your core classes. They are also the ones whom you spend a significant amount of time with during the first semester.

For Adam Miller (Darden, '20), having a diverse team with unique skill sets made the experience inclusive, especially because everyone was able to contribute. There were certain cases in which one of his teammates, an ex-consultant, knew what to do because of his past experience working on that specific business problem. Another teammate had worked in sales and was excellent at synthesizing information and presenting it in a succinct way. However, having a smart and talented team does not solve everything. Study teams can have a love-hate relationship, and sometimes you are at the mercy of the luck of the draw. But, it's just as common for teams to click as it is for them to have issues. Regardless of the team dynamics, any time you spend 12–14 hours a day five days a week with the same people, there are bound to be some issues. Learning to work well with others is a critical skill you will need for the rest of your business career. As the saying goes, misery loves company, and sometimes your study team—whatever your final grade or performance—can provide a good bonding experience through a stressful and challenging time. Miller observed, "I knew our team would be close when the ex-consultant guy started bringing a case of beer every Wednesday for no reason."

In some cases, you will work with people on your team on a specific assignment for which you'll all get the same grade. Other times, you'll be studying together as you prepare for exams and tests. This learning team structure allows you to work with a diverse group of people. While you may not be an expert in accounting, the former accountant on your team can help you through a problem set or key concept that you are struggling with. However, diverse people mean different skills and different work styles, and while you may get along with many people, there are others you may struggle with, at least initially.

SPOTLIGHT: The case method

MBA programs employ a learning technique called the **case method**. The case method is a teaching approach that uses decision-forcing cases to put students in the role of people who were faced with difficult decisions at some point in the past. Under this method, a professor engages students in lively discussions instead of delivering lectures. Each case typically outlines a real business scenario or challenge that a company faced. It presents a set of decisions to be made, and you—as the decision-maker—must analyze the situation and explain what you would do. Prior to class, the teams often meet to discuss the case, analyze the decisions, and talk through how they might respond. While most MBA programs have incorporated the case method into some form of their academic curriculum, at some schools, such as at UVA (Darden), the case method is used throughout the entire academic experience.

During his first year at Darden, Miller experienced the highs and lows of the case method. He found that the method forces students to be prepared for class. Since he knew he might be called on to share his opinion, it forced him to prepare and have a point of view. The challenge with this approach is that the case can be hard to solve and to learn from. According to Miller, "Most people, even those at Darden or HBS, will agree that it doesn't make sense to learn everything with the case method. It presumes that your study group will be able to solve 75%+ of the case without needing help from the professor, but there isn't always the time, patience, or the knowledge in the room to feel ready by the next day."

Fortunately for Miller, he had a learning team. His team would meet regularly for 2.5 hours every night to discuss the cases for the next day. Maureen Keegan (Darden, '17) also found the case method to be a valuable learning approach: "It's more interesting to listen to someone talk about how they used a certain concept in their past job and how it applies in the real world rather than just reading about it in a textbook."

Managing a full academic workload

During the first two quarters, the academic workload can be fairly intense, and not ideal for rest and sleep, especially as students are adjusting to MBA life. Miller felt this in Charlottesville, and during the first two quarters, he was running on about 5.5 hours of sleep, which caused him to gain 10 pounds and have bags under his eyes. He managed to survive the semester and earned high marks with the help of a great support system (his girlfriend). "Given the sheer volume of learning, I often felt like I wasn't fully comprehending the material," observed Miller. Fortunately, his hard work paid off, and he earned excellent grades.

Types of Learning Experiences

Similar to undergraduate programs, lectures, class participation, and assignments are critical components of the academic MBA program. However, MBA programs have recognized that people learn differently and need practical applications. Numerous types of academic learning experiences are offered in full-time MBA programs. To address the need for practical application, many schools have labs, projects, partnerships with businesses, immersion trips, and other forms of applied learning to help students learn concepts and applications.

Global immersion programs

Many MBA programs offer global immersion programs, which allow students to take a course on a particular topic in a specific country or region, to be followed by a field visit at the end of the class. This combines both a traditional class experience (e.g., lecture) with a trip or field study.

For example, with Duke University's Fuqua MBA program, students have the option of participating in GATE, a program in which the politics, economy, and culture of a particular region are taught by professors who are experts in the region. Students spend the term in classroom learning followed by a trip during their spring break.

Field programs and consulting projects

At Fuqua, Shannon Griesser (Fuqua, '19) was interested in exploring careers in social impact. She was able to take advantage of CASEi3 team, an impact investing-focused client project that exposed her to the world of incorporating social impact with financial returns. For Griesser, the chance to get real-world, hands-on experience helped her focus on where within the wide world of social impact she could find her niche.

Combining academic and real-world experiences

During her first year at the University of Michigan, Stephanie Simpson (Ross, '21) participated in MAP, a quarter-long experiential learning class where she and her peers were given a client with a real-life problem, and worked during the quarter to solve it, culminating with a set of recommendations and solutions that they presented to the client. Additionally, Simpson also participated in the Crisis Challenge, an experiential learning program where she and her team were given a company crisis, and each of them was given a role of a different leader (ex: CMO, CFO) and had to respond in the situation. In the simulation, Simpson played the role of the CMO, and was monitoring social media platforms like Twitter to figure out how the company should handle the press and media. Simpson found the real-world nature of both of these programs to be valuable learning experiences. "These experiences gave me a chance to learn in a safe space, and even if I failed, I would be able to get real-time feedback on how to improve," Simpson said.

Applying your Coursework to your Career

Students enjoy the opportunity to learn new skills and gain new knowledge in the classroom, but what they really want is to know that what they are learning is going to help them be successful in their future career choice. Fortunately for many, what is taught in the classroom is directly relevant to their summer internships and full-time jobs.

Core classes provide a strong foundation

During her first year at Yale, Jasmine Ako (Yale SOM ,'19) relied on a number of her core classes that helped her succeed in her summer internship at a global consulting firm, which then propelled her into her current career in a full-time role at the same firm. "Strategy and Marketing provided me with the fundamentals and frameworks which were helpful for assessing different industries and markets, said Ako. Such knowledge was useful due to the project-based nature of consulting where Ako had to get up to speed quickly on a new client, project, or industry. Furthermore, Ako also found some of her elective classes to be valuable to her leadership and soft skill development.

"Classes such as Managing Groups and Team and Power and Politics which focused on people and dynamics within organizations were critical to helping me understand how to navigate team-based situations and organizational cultures," Ako said. "The consulting industry is very different from my pre-MBA industry, and without these courses, it would have been much more challenging to make the transition."

Classes provide confidence to career switchers

Alexandra Jaeggi (Marshall, '20) entered business school with a desire to transition to a new career, but as a former teacher, she knew that she needed a solid business foundation to navigate a new field. During her summer internship as a Product Marketer, Jaeggi put to use her statistics and marketing analytics learnings while working on analyzing complex data sets. She also had to present numerous times throughout her summer to varying audiences, and relied on the feedback and practice of presenting that she got from her Communications class. "My core classes in my first year gave me the confidence to tackle multiple projects during my summer internship, that I didn't have expertise or experience in before business school," Jaeggi said.

Challenging classes lead to new opportunities

Prior to attending business school, Jeff Ellington (Wharton, '17) didn't know what a t-test p-value, or 95% confidence interval was, but after taking Intro to Statistics during his first year it opened his eyes to statistical thinking. In the end, he ended up taking over eight statistics-related courses throughout his MBA.

"I decided to lean in and try and learn a new challenging subject in business school because I was interested in stretching and growing myself," Ellington said. "Furthermore, I had incredible instructors, and wanted to take advantage of that opportunity that I knew would be hard to find again after I graduated." For him, the coursework ended up paying off. During his second year of business school, he built a thesis and 30-slide pitch deck on Artificial Intelligence that landed him a job at a Venture Capital Firm. And now, in his role leading a product team at a growing startup, he is using the concepts from those classes to test and learn to build better user experiences. "I'm grateful that business school gave me the opportunity and support to learn something hard, as it's paid off."

Applied learning opportunities provide real-world experience

During her second year of school, Kellie Braam (Booth, '18) took "New Products Lab," where she and 3 other classmates were paired with a company on a project to develop new innovation. Braam's team was paired with Hershey's who was trying to develop a new low-calorie ice cream product. In addition to getting a chance to collaborate in a team environment on a real project with her peers, Braam found partnering with an industry leader like Hershey's to be a valuable experience. "Getting a chance to work with a real company on a real idea gave me great exposure to the product and innovation development process in the CPG industry. Now that I work in this industry, I feel confident and can ask the right questions when I work with marketers and product development team members as a result of taking this class," Braam said.

How Do you Take Full Advantage of your Academic Experience?

Considering the assortment of core classes and electives, study and learning teams, group projects, hands-on learning, case studies, and everything else, how do you make the best use of your academic experience while in business school?

Find your learning goals

Like most things in life, if you can define your goals, it can help anchor you in a strategy to make the most of your academic coursework. Najee Johnson (UNC Kenan-Flager, '15) used this approach while he was a student at UNC Kenan-Flagler. As a former teacher, Johnson deeply valued the academic experience. He wanted to balance immersing himself in learning the material with being cognizant of the time constraints. He understood that people only have the capacity to learn so much, especially in a short amount of time. To put this into action, Johnson focused on his core classes, especially the ones that would help him prepare for his desired track of management consulting. In addition to learning the concepts in the classroom, he made sure to pay attention to the stories from his classmates, which married the theoretical to the practical experience.

Learn how you learn best

Some people love listening to lectures. Others appreciate more team-based assignments collaborating with others. And some like the real-world application of an immersion class, or class where you can work directly on a consulting type assignment or project with a business. Regardless of what type of learner you are, figuring out how you learn best and then identifying the environment or structure that suits you best can set you up for success. For John Huang, (Ross, '15) working on group projects was very similar to the project-based nature of management consulting and offered him the best environment to absorb and learn new concepts and fundamentals in addition to understanding how to manage different team dynamics. By understanding the learning environments where you can learn best, you can proactively identify the opportunities where these exist, and maximize your learning experience.

Learn how to learn

As a former consultant, Nick Johnson (NYU Stern, '15), was used to being thrown into a situation with a new client in a new industry that he had never worked in and getting up to speed fast to ensure he could contribute to the client engagement. So, when he was in business school and was put in a situation where he had to learn a new academic subject or a new concept, his ability to learn quickly was instrumental to his own learning and development. Johnson understood that it would be difficult to learn every single concept in every single class. Instead, his approach was to obtain a fundamental understanding that would enable him to participate in class and then rely on other resources later to augment his learning as needed. "It's impossible to expect yourself to learn an entirely new subject in three short months, but if you can pick up the fundamentals and augment it with real-world examples or insights from your classmates, you can start to connect the dots," said Johnson.

Learn for the future

As the world continues to go through lots of change driven by technological advances, in order for companies and employees to keep up with the pace of change they must continuously acquire new skills and experiences. As such, the most successful companies and employers in the future will be the ones who can learn fast, acquire new skills, and evolve as times change. As Kelly Palmer, Chief Learning Officer of Degreed, an online learning platform notes, "One of the most important skills is being an agile learner."

Since you'll need to learn and build new skills as you evolve and grow your career, using part of your time in business school to "learn how to learn" is a worthwhile endeavor. Developing both a desire and process for acquiring new skills will position you well not just for class performance but also for knowledge and skill acquisition needed throughout your career.

At school, you'll have the chance to create a learning journey that is unique to your interests. You will likely find that your interest in particular subjects increases during your time at school. And, while it won't be possible for you to learn everything, one of the best gifts an MBA program can provide is a commitment to learning. Whether it's in the classroom, or at your job, your academic experience can inspire you with the desire to keep learning for the rest of your life so you can continue to acquire knowledge and new skills, long after your courses end.

STUDENT STORIES: LESSONS FROM THE FRONT LINE

There is so much that you can learn once you adjust to the academic environment. These students share their perspectives on how they navigated the academic experience in business school.

Moving from Teacher to Student

by Najee Johnson (UNC Kenan-Flagler, '15)

After starting his career as a teacher, Najee Johnson enrolled in business school to pivot to a career in management consulting. Drawing on his experiences as a teacher, Johnson used his teaching expertise to navigate the academic experience during his first year. He shared his approach, and his tips for success. Transitioning back into the classroom.

Transitioning back into the classroom

It had only been a few years since graduation, but it still took time to get back into the academic mindset. Participating in UNC's Analytical Skills Workshop prior to classes starting eased the transition, especially as I lacked a formal background in statistics, economics, and accounting. Taking short introductory classes on these topics taught by professors gave me a solid foundation for starting off right.

At UNC, I took the same core classes with my section and my study team. Since we had diverse backgrounds, we were all able to learn from one another. Classmates from outside my study team who shared my learning interests were valuable, especially near exam time. We studied together, teaching and coaching one another, and helping with catch-up when needed.

Lots to learn

As a former teacher, I watched as professors dealt with the challenge of covering a wide range of content in a compressed manner. As a student, this meant being thrown multiple new concepts or topics at once and figuring out how to make sense of them and then apply them to an assignment, test, or project. This was challenging at times, and during those moments I reminded myself that I couldn't learn *everything* in a short three months. Instead, I broke down concepts into smaller steps and reinforced what I learned by working through practice problems.

Learning to prioritize

Business school is one big prioritization exercise. For management consulting recruitment, I knew I would need a certain GMAT score, but also that I had to focus my energy on the right classes that employers would want to make sure I did well in. There were also company info sessions, coffee chats, and other relevant events after school hours which limited time with my study team, so I shared my priorities with the team from the outset. I wanted to do well enough in my classes to show my analytical horsepower, but I knew I couldn't necessarily get the best grade in every single class. It wasn't easy, but having clear priorities meant I could make adjustments and honor all of my commitments.

Final advice

COMMUNICATE PRIORITIES

It's important to not only know your priorities but also to share them with your study team so that you can find ways to contribute while honoring your priorities.

USE YOUR RESOURCES

Furthermore, don't be afraid to ask for help! You'll be surrounded by smart, hard-working individuals, whether they're former accountants who can help you read a balance sheet or a former marketer who understands how the 4Ps actually work in the real world. Leveraging the diverse talents of those around you not only helps you learn but adds to the richness of the MBA experience.

How to Navigate the Transition Back into the Academic Environment

by Emily Moore (Anderson, '20)

After spending years in NYC in the media industry Emily Moore moved to the west coast to attend UCLA Anderson. While the climate changed, Moore's familiarity with the hustle and bustle of NYC prepared her to tackle the many challenges of business school, and she shared her advice about transitioning back into the academic world.

After almost 4 years in New York City, I packed my bags and moved to LA to attend UCLA Anderson. My New York life prepared me well for business school as I worked long hours in New York, traveling often for work, and was just used to the go-go-go. The act of being busy continued in business school, but just in a different way. The biggest change of going back to school from work is that I'm actually only in class 9-12 hours per week instead of being at work for 60+. Theoretically, I would have more free time in business school, but I definitely didn't. Instead, I just have more of a choice on how I spend those non-class hours—studying, attending recruiting events, or preparing for interviews, planning or attending a club event and being social.

Life at Anderson

At UCLA Anderson, we are on the quarter system and as first years, we started at the beginning of August, had a five-week summer quarter and then started the fall quarter at the end of September. During the fall quarter, a typical day included Marketing on Mondays and Wednesdays for 1.5 hours, Economics and Data + Decisions both for 1.5 hours on Tuesdays and Thursdays and the Parker Career Series on Mondays for 1.5 hours. I would be on campus for 8-10+ hours most Mondays through Thursdays, but would not typically come to campus on Fridays.

Balancing the opportunities and demands of business school

Even though I was focused on doing well in the classroom, there were other aspects of the MBA program that were important to me as well. Outside of the classroom, the highlight of my fall quarter was getting involved in the Admissions Ambassador Corps (AAC). I applied for and was selected to be a Director of the organization, which meant that I would take on a role as an ambassador for the school. This entailed taking prospective students on campus tours, to class visits and connecting with them on the phone or for a coffee chat on campus. Doing this meant that I needed to prioritize and manage my time effectively. For example, my first class every day started at 9:45 am so I would get up around 5:30- 6:00 am (I'm a morning person!) and either go for a run or study and read for class. I'd get to school around 9:30 and then head to my first class. The 11:30 am-12:30 pm block usually involved a company presentation over lunch or a club event. In the afternoon, I'd go to class, and meet up with my learning team for various case assignments and projects. At night, I would either attend a company presentation event or study at home. This made for long days or spending weekends focusing on work instead of being social, but because I got a lot of value and meaning out of these activities, I was happy with the trade-offs I was making.

Final advice

DON'T FORGET PERSONAL TIME

This was the first time I lived in a different time zone from my family and most of my friends. Most of them are on the east coast and while 3 hours doesn't seem like a big difference, it actually is. I pride myself on being good at keeping in touch with my friends and family—usually by phone calls and texts when we are not living in the same city. I would often leave campus at 7:00 or 8:00 pm and it would be too late to call the east coast during the week. After a while, I decided to try to find time during my afternoon or when I was driving to/from campus to call them. I'm still working on it, but it's important to use the 15 free minutes that I sometimes have in the afternoon to make a phone call. I make a conscious effort to call at least one friend or family member per day.

Building the Business Skill Set through the Academic Experience

by Iman Nanji (Anderson, '20)

Iman Nanji entered the dual-degree program at UCLA Anderson with a desire to work at the intersection of the public and private sectors. She knew that developing her business acumen was important to this goal, and she focused on building these skills through her coursework and classes. In this essay, she describes using the academic experience to achieve her career goals.

My path to UCLA Anderson

I always planned to attend graduate school and took the GRE just after completing my undergraduate studies, but I wasn't sure if I would go back to business school or do another professional degree. I have always been interested in the intersection of policy and business, and after working in the Financial Services and Social Sector, I saw what can be achieved when the public and private sectors work together, and decided to apply to business school.

The transition back to school

Transitioning back into the academic environment at UCLA Anderson was tough. There was little consistency in my schedule and lots of homework, so my weekends were no longer my own. Luckily, my first year was at the public policy school, so once I got to business school, I was familiar with writing papers, studying, and taking tests. My favorite class was my strategy class, which helped me think through frameworks for interviews and will be useful for my summer internship. Operations was the most challenging class because I was starting at zero. To foster collaboration throughout the academic experience, UCLA Anderson assigned us to learning teams, and I loved mine because of their varied skill sets. The team's openness to mutual support was crucial during busy times in my internship.

Using internships to spur learning

During my first year at business school, I worked on my capstone project in the public policy school, and I had a fellowship through the public policy program to work at the Los Angeles Mayor's office for 20 hours a week. This experience aligned with my interests and also gave me the chance to develop skills I knew I needed for my summer internship. At times it felt nearly impossible to do everything, but I was very deliberate about prioritizing my commitments and ensuring that everything was helping me work toward my career goals. With my capstone project, I decided to work with a team of women that I trusted and I knew would be understanding of my hectic schedule. I was honest and communicative with them, and they were flexible with me, letting me call into meetings and work on my sections in my own time.

Final advice

MANAGE THE FOUR "BUCKETS"

Before I started, a friend advised me to prioritize my school activities—academic, social, recruiting, and extracurricular—and I decided to focus on recruiting during the first two quarters. I declined social events when they impacted recruiting, rushed through some academic assignments when I had to prep for interviews, and only focused on relevant extracurricular activities.

FOCUS

Work piles up quickly, so stay on top of it. Classes are fast-paced (especially in the quarter system), and if you miss any it's easy to fall behind. School is different from work, so don't expect lots of free time because you have to juggle many different responsibilities in addition to classwork.

Making the Most of the MBA Academic Experience at Darden

by Maureen Keegan (Darden, '15)

Entering Darden as a career-switcher, Maureen Keegan was eager to get back into the classroom and round out her business skill set. Through Darden's case method and core experience, Keegan was able to build a strong foundation of business fundamentals.

The first few weeks of business school were an absolute whirlwind, but "Darden Before Darden," a 10-day pre-matriculation program, helped ease the transition. Before classes started, I had time to settle into my apartment, get used to the schedule, meet some of my classmates, and see how busy school was going to be. Orientation took another three days, with introductions to clubs and activities, a mock case, and career discovery workshops.

We were split into five sections and all took the same classes, Monday through Thursday, from August through mid-March. Our learning teams were formed across the sections, so they included people from all different backgrounds. We typically met for a couple of hours in the evening, Sunday through Wednesday, to go over our cases for the next day, and so we came to know each other really well.

Getting back into the classroom

As an International Studies major in college, and having worked in a non-profit before school, I came in with very little business background, so I learned something new in almost every class. The case method required us to figure things out on our own before class, and that took some getting used to. It was great to learn from the professional experiences of my classmates—it was more interesting than just reading a textbook.

In the first quarter, Accounting and Decision Analysis were definitely the classes in which I felt I was learning the most, but my favorite Q1 class was Decision Analysis. Each class built on the previous ones, so we went from doing basic decision trees on the first day to creating Crystal Ball models in the final classes. The professor somehow made intimidating content easy to understand.

In the second quarter, I learned the newest material in the continuation of Accounting. There was also Finance and another new class, Operations, which I enjoyed, thanks largely to a really engaging professor who made figuring out process optimization feel like detective work. I discovered how closely connected the different subjects can be, with lots of crossovers.

Final advice

FOCUS WHERE YOU GIVE 100%

It's important to remember: it's impossible to give 100% to everything, but for the things that are important, it's important to give 100%!

TREASURE YOUR WEEKENDS

I tried to use the weekend as a chance to check-in. Did I drop the ball during the week? What would next week look like? Could I use this week to make next week easier? It's a juggling act!

Key Takeaways

The chance to get back into the classroom to learn and grow is exciting. To make the most of the experience of learning and developing new skills, consider the following:

IDENTIFY HOW YOU LEARN BEST

Figure out the best learning mechanism for you. Whether that's in the classroom, in your study team, or through hands-on learning, figure out where you learn best.

SHARE YOUR PRIORITIES WITH YOUR LEARNING OR STUDY TEAM

Be upfront with your team about your priorities.

CONTRIBUTE AND LISTEN TO YOUR PEERS

The ability to learn from the experiences of your peers is a unique aspect of the MBA experience. Find opportunities to do this as much as you can, and make sure that you are sharing your own experiences too.

ALIGN COURSEWORK TO YOUR CAREER INTERESTS

Spend time aligning your courses to your career interests to maximize your career goals.

MAKE SPACE FOR CURIOSITY

Make room for a few that spark your curiosity as well. You may not get this kind of learning opportunity again.

Key Questions to Answer

- What classes are most important to my internship/career aspirations?
- How do you feel about grades? How important are they to you and your career?

- When working on teams, what is your work style? What roles/responsibilities play to your strengths?

CHAPTER FOUR

CAREERS AND RECRUITING

Identifying your future career path and finding that summer internship are both exciting and daunting. This chapter will cover how students of all interests, backgrounds, and goals identify their next career move and go after it.

Everyone is Still Figuring it Out

After moving from San Francisco to New York to attend NYU, Charlie Mangiardi (NYU Stern, '17) was excited but nervous about entering school. He wanted to switch careers, to one in which he had no experience while dealing with peers who already had an advantage.

"I assumed that everyone here would have it all figured out. While some did, there were many students who were using this time to assess other career opportunities." Mangiardi continued, "The reality is that there is not a lot of time in business school, so the more time you have to spend on finding your path, the less time you have for other things which are also important, so it's important to be diligent but focused."

Transitioning careers in business school

According to a study conducted by Transparent MBA, 87% of MBAs switch either functions or industries in their jobs directly before and after B-school. Some 69% switch both functions and industries. Individuals using a full-time MBA from an elite B-school to accelerate their current career paths are in the significant minority. These statistics confirm the notion that Business school has long been seen as a platform to switch your career. Whether that's a function, industry, or a combination of both, the advantage of a well-rounded MBA degree is that it gives you the chance to position yourself for something you previously were not doing.

Some MBA students come into school with a clear mindset of what they want to transition to after they graduate. Others are less sure, and use their time in business school to explore their ideas and aspirations. But even for those who have an idea of what they want to do, the beauty of business school is that fresh perspectives and insights can emerge through exposure to new fields and opportunities and can often shift your focus.

Even if you know what you want, it's still a lot of work

Prior to entering business school, Tony Morash (UNC Kenan-Flagler, '16) knew he wanted to pursue a career in management consulting, and doing so meant that he was going to have to work extra hard early on to stand out in the recruiting process. Morash was clear on what he wanted to achieve, but managing the networking opportunities, company presentations, and interview preparation were still challenging and demanding. "It caused me to focus and prioritize," Morash said.

Even when you find out what you want, other paths emerge

Upon entering Fuqua's MBA program, Winny Anradini (Fuqua, '19) did her research and identified that she wanted to move into a career in social impact. After the first few months of networking and working with the career center, she realized that while her passion for social impact had not wavered, the opportunities were usually on a just-in-time basis, and many of the institutions appreciated candidates with more experience. As a result, she decided to pivot to another path. Even though she was ultimately successful, the shift wasn't without its challenges.

Exploring your career options

Since recruiting starts early, MBA Programs provide resources and programming during the beginning of the program to help students quickly identify the areas they want to focus on in pursuit of a summer internship. These workshops, classes, and events offer students deep dives into a function or industry and are taught by Career Management Coaches and Professionals, some of whom have past business experience in these fields. Furthermore, events with alums and practitioners are often brought to campus to provide insight into what their job and careers look like. During her first year in business school, Kellie Braam (Booth, '18) did her research, identified her chosen industry and function and built a list of companies that she was interested in. On a whim, Braam heard that a company that wasn't on her target list was hosting a "lunch and learn" session with a handful of alums. While the company wasn't initially on her list, she enjoyed the presentation and the alums she met, and she eventually applied for the internship and ended up interning there for the summer.

Finding your right path through exploration

A significant element of exploring career options focuses on self-reflection and awareness. Whether you're entering business school to make the switch to a new career or you already know what you want to do after graduation, the schools focus on helping you to understand your skills and interests and to build a plan towards that path. This often starts with reflection and self-discovery. Through various introspection exercises, assessments, and exploration of opportunities, you begin to identify some potential career paths. Finding your next career also involves researching and learning from others. This is where networking (as previously discussed) is important, as talking to alums, or fellow students about their experiences and careers is often a great way to discern if a specific career might be right for you.

How much time do you have to really explore?

Business school gives you an opportunity to hit pause and identify where you want to go next. In the recruiting and marketing process for MBA applicants, many schools play up the notion that this is a great time to explore your interests and passions, which is partially true. In business school, you do have plenty of opportunities to find out where you want to take your career, but how much time do you actually have to "figure it out" with respect to recruiting? This question is especially relevant if you are interested in industries like consulting and investment banking, where recruiting starts so early that if you are on the fence you can easily fall behind.

After working in leadership development at a small consulting firm prior to business school, Griesser pivoted to a career in Sustainability and Social Impact at an international non-profit organization. While many students like Griesser are able to explore their options and pivot their careers, it is not always as cut-and-dried.

Griesser entered business school with the assumption that she would have time to explore different career opportunities, build her skills, and find the path that was right for her. But because recruiting started so early, the time she had to explore was shorter than expected. In addition, many companies are interested in hiring MBA students, but they are also interested in selecting students who already have the skills or experiences they are looking for. To make this work, Griesser used any opportunity she had to learn about different industries, functions, or roles. This involved grabbing lunch with students in her sections who worked in areas she was interested in or getting them to connect her to people in their network to explore it further. "Switching careers is absolutely possible, but it does take focus and discipline because there are so many priorities coming at you at once," said Griesser.

SPOTLIGHT: Career exploration guidance from a career expert

As a Career Director for Technology at Duke University's Fuqua MBA Program, Michael Wong advises and coaches hundreds of students each year through their career exploration. Wong offered these tips for how to effectively use your career exploration time to identify a career path that fits your goals.

Lock it down in the first term

According to Wong, students should solidify their direction by the end of the first quarter or by the end of their first term, "Students should ideally get to a place where they are focused on 1-2 industries and within those industries, they should aim for between 1-2 functional areas."

Focus is better than generalization

While MBA programs give students the ability to explore many different career paths, Wong believes that focus is critical to success. "The more focused students can be, the better they will come across to potential hiring managers and alumni. The broader their interests are, the more difficult it will be for them to have a focused message that sounds convincing," Wong said.

Use self-reflection to get unstuck

Sometimes, students have a hard time figuring out what they want to do, and that's perfectly normal. To get unstuck, Wong encourages students to think about professional experiences where they have lost all sense of time and where they felt they were in the zone. "What were they doing at that time? Were they leading a team, developing an innovative solution during a tight deadline, mentoring a co-worker going through a difficult time?"

Consider taking personality examinations

Wong encourages his students to take professional or personality tests, such as Strengths Finder or the DISC Assessment. According to Wong, "These exams, insights and experiences should help start an inventory of the types of experiences that should be included in a career." From there, he then encourages his students to take these insights and get feedback from other peers and alums. "Oftentimes, when you can share these insights with others, they can point out which functional areas or industries might align best with your interests," Wong said.

The First-Year Summer Internship Recruiting Process

Regardless of who you are, and whether you know what you want to do, the recruiting and career exploration is critical to the MBA experience. This section covers a number of key elements of the process that ring true for everyone.

Recruiting starts early

Time and time again, students remark on how surprised they are at how early the recruiting process starts. Recruiting starts the minute you walk on campus, as many companies will already have presentations, office hours, and coffee chats on your school's academic calendar. Some schools do try to limit these activities through rules that govern when companies can come onto campus (e.g., not until after a certain day/date), but the reality is that even if you are at a school with such policies you'll want to start figuring out your career goals and aspirations very early on. This process certainly varies in duration from one student to the next, but the earlier you start, the better positioned you will be.

Shannon Griesser (Fuqua '19) was thoughtful about reflecting on and articulating her goals and aspirations for what she wanted to get out of her business school experience, and she also knew from a career perspective that she wanted to get into the Social Impact sector. She even took the time to prepare her elevator pitch and network with peers before entering to give her a leg up. But what she wasn't as prepared for was just how early the recruiting process started. As she observed, "Recruiting starts the moment you set foot on campus if not earlier, it's important to be mindful of that."

This sentiment is true, especially for tried and true MBA sectors like consulting and investment banking. Students who choose to recruit in those industries usually start recruiting right when school starts, and they have immediate deliverables or deadlines.

The important "deliverables"

Throughout the recruiting process, you'll often rely on a number of key deliverables as you network, apply to firms, and set up interviews. Making sure that your deliverables are in tip-top shape, comply with school standards, and that they differentiate themselves takes time but pays off. If you're looking to get ahead, consider focusing on some of the most common ones:

RESUME

You'll need this for every job or internship you apply to. Your school will give you guidelines on how you should construct your resume, so make sure to follow and comply with their standards.

COVER LETTER

Many roles still require you to write a personalized cover letter for the internship or job. Your school will have some guidelines and best practices on what to write.

LINKEDIN PROFILE

LinkedIn is ubiquitous, especially when it comes to careers and professional networking. Make sure your profile is up to date, accurate, and features a great headshot.

ELEVATOR PITCH

You'll have hundreds of conversations during your first year in which you'll need to explain who you are and what you are interested in. Taking some time to learn how to tell a succinct but compelling story of your history and what you're looking to do next is a worthwhile use of time given how much you'll be using this.

NETWORKING EMAILS

Throughout your recruiting, you'll constantly be connecting with recruiters, alumni, and professionals at companies you are interested in. While you'll need to tailor your email to each individual person, creating a few standard templates based on the type of email (e.g., follow-up, thank you, informational interview request) can often save you time.

On-campus recruiting

If you attend a top MBA program, you will find that employers will be actively searching for candidates in your school. These employers participate in on-campus recruiting, in which they formally work with your career center to recruit students. This typically happens with larger companies that have an established presence and relationship with your school. Examples include consulting firms, investment banks, or traditional leadership development programs. During the fall, representatives and alumni from these companies will come on campus with formal company presentations, networking events, and workshops. As mentioned, this is especially true for traditional MBA paths such as consulting and investment banking. If you plan on recruiting for these industries you will most likely spend time at these events.

Off-campus recruiting

While most schools have many companies that come on campus formally, there are lots of companies out there that don't formally recruit on campus. These companies recruit off-campus, which means they are out there and looking, but it's up to you to find them. The path of least resistance is often on-campus recruiting; off-campus recruiting is much more intensive and student-driven, but it also offers more potential opportunities, provided you have the patience and persistence to find them. Furthermore, off-campus roles are often just-in-time, or at least in the first year. They are available fairly late in the year (April–May), which sometimes makes students nervous, given how close that is to the end of the first year. While this can be a risk, it's also a fairly common practice, especially for specific industries or functions such as venture capital, technology, or non-profit. Since off-campus recruiting is more diverse in nature, if you pursue this route you need to be more directive and in control of your career search. While this requires a student to take ownership and really drive the process, it also allows for greater flexibility for a student to identify an opportunity that fits your unique needs.

SPOTLIGHT: Common recruiting timelines by industry or function

Every industry or function has a unique timeline for the recruiting process for both internships and full-time opportunities. While these will vary, here are some general guidelines for common industries and functions:

Consulting

Consulting firms recruit largely on campus and in general, they adhere to a fixed schedule. Companies that recruit on-campus typically allow students to start applying in the fall and inform them in Early December/January if they receive an interview. It's not uncommon for your Christmas holiday to be filled with interview prep. Internship hiring starts in January, but don't be fooled into complacency — you should be networking and prepping for case interviews well before the new year in this competitive field. Full-time offers center around the end of the summer internship in August, and at the peak of second-year recruiting in October and November.

Investment Banking

Investment Banking recruiting is unique because investment banks like to convert their interns into full-time employees. Therefore, there are not many second-year recruitment opportunities. If you decide as a first-year that you want to get into investment banking, you will likely spend October, November, and December networking and interviewing. By January you'll have an offer, a few if you're lucky, or you'll come up empty-handed—in which case you'll still have plenty of time to recruit for other industries.

Technology

For many programs, a lot of recruiting for tech internships will be off-campus, which generally extends from January-May. This "just-in-time" hiring approach means that if you are recruiting for technology, you'll be looking for full-time opportunities throughout that entire time at business school.

Marketing

On-campus recruiting for Marketing roles usually is split between two key tracks: CPG and Brand Marketing, and then Tech Marketing. CPG and Brand Marketing tend to recruit mostly on campus at top MBA Programs, and start coming to campus in the early fall, while formally conducting interviews in early January-February. For example, Bryce Parrish (UNC Kenan-Flagler, '16) started engaging with CPG companies in early September but locked in an internship in February. For Tech Marketing, many firms recruit off-campus or just in time, which basically means that it is on a rolling basis with an emphasis on the February, March, and April time frame. As the impact of tech companies continues to grow, more and more firms recruit on campus. This has moved up the timeline for tech hiring.

Networking: A Dirty Word, but it Doesn't Have to Be

If you say the word, "networking" around a group of MBA students, you'll often get some eye-rolls. Most students know that networking is a critical and perhaps trite and overused word to describe what you do in business school, but that doesn't mean it's not important. According to Dorie Clark, Adjunct Professor at Duke University's Fuqua MBA Program and author of *Stand Out Networking*, networking doesn't have to feel dirty. "It's not about making shallow, insincere connections and filling your wallet with business cards. Instead, the real goal is to turn brief encounters into mutually-beneficial and lasting friendships—in both your personal and professional life."

You may have chosen your school because of the networking opportunities, or you may have been given the advice to "network" as it pertains to the job search. Regardless, the word networking is synonymous with business school, and it tends to have a negative connotation, sometimes deservedly so. But here's the reality: very few people, in general, have the ability to find a new job or career without the help or assistance of other people. It truly does "take a village." MBA programs provide that "village" through an expansive network of alumni, employers, faculty, administrators, all made available to you for your own career journey.

Adam Miller (Darden, '20) learned the value of networking even before stepping foot at Darden. In previous work experience, Miller's department was eliminated, and he had to search for job opportunities in various parts of the company. This was a humbling but rewarding experience, as it allowed him to meet talented people in various functions and ultimately land him a role he never would have found on his own. Armed with this positive experience, Miller approached networking in a similar manner when he got to Darden—he used it as a way to learn about people's unique careers, ask them questions to gather information, and build relationships in case there might be opportunities down the road.

Nick Johnson (NYU Stern, '15) found networking to be extremely valuable to his search for a management consulting internship. While many of the firms he was interested in had similarities, there were nuances to them that he could only understand by talking directly to these firms and their NYU alumni. For example, he learned how the consultant staffing model differed between two firms: one had a national approach and the other had an office or regional strategy. This information could only be gained by speaking with the Stern alumni at these companies: "The granular insights not only give you a good perspective but developing a network of people who could vouch for you when it came time to review your application was very important."

Networking can be intimidating, especially if you've never done it before

For some, networking might be a foreign concept (it is not common in some cultures), or it might feel awkward or uncomfortable. After spending seven years in the Merchant Marine Academy in India, Ravi Maniar (UNC Kenan-Flagler, '17) embarked on his MBA journey at the University of North Carolina. Throughout his time at UNC, but particularly in recruiting, networking helped him to achieve success. Despite this, Maniar understands that networking is sometimes a foreign idea to international students: "International students, particularly those from Asia, are very adept at social connections and working as a team, but when the same skills must be deployed in a professional setting they find it harder to execute." Maniar added that due to the hierarchical nature of workplace culture in some Asian countries, it can be harder for students from these countries to network casually with recruiters, or sometimes even with some of their classmates, who are more comfortable with these activities. Fortunately, Maniar was able to break through these barriers to find success. His advice: "Flipping the intended purpose of networking from one seeking opportunities to one of learning about opportunities can make networking feel a lot more natural." He added, "It is less awkward to connect with someone you do not know to ask for advice and insights than to ask for a job."

Andrés Romero (McDonough, '19) moved from Santiago, Chile to Washington, D.C., and throughout his time at Georgetown, he saw that students from countries outside the United States who had not been exposed to networking struggled with it initially but adjusted over time. According to Romero, "Concepts such as networking are new to many international students, as we are accustomed to other types of dynamics in the job search." He recalled a particular conversation with a fellow classmate from Mexico who was recruiting for investment banking and had to travel every week to New York to meet with alumni and companies. When asked why he was doing that, his friend said, "Basically, to hang out with people that might hire me." While most students won't be getting on an airplane to go to New York every week, the spirit of what his classmate was doing, in terms of getting to know and build relationships with people who may hire him, is something almost all students will do during their career search.

SPOTLIGHT: Career and recruiting guidance for international students

Reinaldo Carevallas (UNC Kenan-Flager, '19) and Nisthanth Kadiyala (UNC Kenan-Flagler, '16) moved to Chapel Hill from their respective countries to pursue career opportunities in the United States. During their time, they used these best practices in order to achieve their goal of finding a career in the United States.

Take advantage of all of the resources

In addition to working with the Career Clubs and Career Management Center, Carevallas suggests to take advantage of extra resources, such as Diversity recruiting conferences (ex: ROMBA, or NBMBAA.) They have specific positions where there are potential opportunities.

Build a company list

Carevallas also encourages students to build a company list. On that list, he suggests that you include companies that:

- hire on-campus that hire international students;
- hire on conferences that hire international students;
- hire off-campus that hire international students;
- are your dream company but don't hire international students.

From the list above, you should concentrate 70% of your time on the first two, 20% on the third and only 10% on the last one

Expand your network

Kadiyala realized early on that establishing and expanding his network was the key to becoming successful. However, networking is a two-way street. "It was important that I added value to these contacts as much as they did to me. By learning more about what they are working on, and identifying ways I could add value to their work where possible, I built some valuable relationships over time and made that part of my personal brand."

Take internships to build experience

Kandiyala took part-time internships to not only build on his experience but also establish meaningful relationships that helped him secure job opportunities. He identified internships that were in industries and verticals within Tech that were aligned to his interests and strengths, such as cloud software and identity management, and used these internships to add to his experience base. This paid off, as in his second year, he had companies reaching out to him to interview for roles.

SPOTLIGHT: H1B guidance

The H1B is a work visa in the United States that allows for temporary work authorization for special industries and functions and is the visa that most international MBA students need in order to work in the United States. Nishanth Kadiyala (UNC Kenan-Flagler, '16,) was able to secure H1B sponsorship after coming to the United States from India and provided his tips for fellow International students.

Choose the right program

Since the H1B is based on a lottery system, Kadiyala believes it's important to give yourself as many shots as possible to get selected in the lottery. With an MBA, unfortunately, you only get one year of work authorization, meaning only one or two shots at the H1B lottery. To overcome this, some MBA programs, such as the ones at the University of Rochester and Duke University, are offering an MBA with a STEM focus that gives you three years of work authorization instead of one, thereby increasing your chances of securing the visa. During this time, known as the Optional Practical Training (OPT) period, students can work on a student visa, and have the opportunity to apply for a visa multiple times each year.

Choose the right company

According to Kadiyala, many companies with a global footprint already have established processes in place to navigate the visa challenges. He advises students to speak to employers about what they have done to deal with other international employees in the past, and what resources they have that might be able to help. Furthermore, Kadiaya also encourages students to check out non-profits, as they can secure H1B without needing to go through the lottery process.

There are Plenty of Resources for you

If it seems like there is a lot to learn about recruiting, there is! But relax—regardless of whether or not you know what you want to do, MBA programs are structured to assist you in your recruiting and career search. You'll find access to helpful resources, programs, and experiences along the way

Career management center

Each MBA program has a career management center with expert coaches and advisors who can work with you one-on-one to identify internships and full-time opportunities. These career centers also provide workshops, training, and coursework to help achieve your career aspirations. For example, Ava Kavelle (Anderson, '20), in addition to working with her Career Advisor on streamlining her company list against a set of criteria, also used the interview resources, including a repository of past interview questions at the Parker Career Center to prepare for her internship interviews.

Second-year students

Second-year students are invaluable resources for first-year students. Since second-year students were first-year students, they can often provide insights and guidance with a perspective based on their experience. Shannon Griesser (Fuqua, '19) practiced interviewing with a number of second-year students not only to help her nail down tough interview questions but also to refine her story and pitch. Getting feedback from people who had successfully navigated the recruiting process at companies she was applying to was helpful as she went through her own recruiting.

Career clubs

Career clubs and student organizations provide many resources to students who are navigating the recruiting process for internships and full-time offers. In addition to providing networking opportunities by hosting events with employers and alumni, they also offer guidance and coaching. During her first year, Ava Kavelle (Anderson, '20) utilized the AnderTech (Anderson Tech Career Club) especially when it came to interview prep. The club provides many resources, events, and networking opportunities that strengthened her confidence in her interviewing abilities, while also exposing her to the ins and outs of specific companies, functions, and roles. Another valuable event put on by the club were D48s (Dinner for 8) which were small dinners with local alumni where they could learn and get to know alum in specific industries in an intimate setting. Finally, the interview workshops and prep sessions that AnderTech hosted taught Kavelle how to effectively prepare for an interview and successfully execute an interview.

Career fairs, conferences, and events

In addition to the various resources, your school will provide you with recruiting opportunities. There are many conferences, career fairs, and events where you'll get the chance to find internships or full-time positions. Conferences provide a great forum to get in front of employers who are looking to hire summer interns (and in some cases, full-time positions). Two popular conferences are the National Black MBA conference (NBMBA) and the Reaching Out MBA Conference (ROMBA). At these conferences, employers and organizers who share the same mission and values come together and give students a chance to learn more about the roles at the specific companies through a career fair and networking events. Furthermore, they also give students the chance to interview for internships and full-time roles.

SPOTLIGHT: How to use career resources in your MBA program

MBA programs provide numerous resources to help students navigate the recruiting process. Here is an example of how Kirsten Smith (UNC Kenan-Flager, '20) used the resources.

Career clubs and treks

Smith found it helpful to review the websites and briefings of companies that she was interested in, before going to company events or speaking with alum at those companies. "They helped me understand their core values and mission statements and ensure that I was aligned with their culture and goals." Furthermore, Smith participated in a career trek organized by UNC's Business Technology club to Seattle and the San Francisco Bay Area to visit nine companies over fall break. "That was an extremely helpful trip to see the office spaces firsthand, feel the culture, and try to envision yourself in the setting." After returning home, Smith "wrote down the first word that came to my mind about each of them and had two friends do the same so that we really thought about the impression the company had left on us."

Second-year students

Smith met with her assigned career coach, a second-year student, on a tri-weekly to monthly basis to ensure she was on the right path with regard to recruiting. "I sought feedback on my resume, cover letter, and interview stories. I also worked with my career coach to identify other students or alumni that I could network with, to get a better understanding of a specific role or insight into a company that I was interested in."

Career management center and career resources

Finally, Smith also utilized UNC's Business Communication Center, where she was able to work with interview preparation coaches. "This preparation was vital to succeeding in the interview process, and the feedback from coaches was helpful to learning how to improve my interview skills." Smith also leveraged the Career and Leadership office at UNC, as a way to "gut check" her company list, the types of internships that she was applying for, and to gather intel on the on-campus interview process for the various companies she was interviewing with.

"Based on my experience, our Career and Leadership office is as helpful as you choose to make it. I felt that in order to get the most out of my sessions, I needed to come prepared with companies and functional areas in mind and have a clear sense of the content of my resume, cover letter, and behavioral interview responses," Smith said.

Navigating Career Transitions

As stated earlier, many students come to business school with a desire to transition into a new career. While this is normal and expected, transitioning to a new career isn't as simple as choosing your career—it requires thinking about how your own skills and experiences and goals make you a great candidate for a new chosen field or opportunity, and then successfully conveying that to recruiters and hiring managers throughout the interview process. A term you'll hear in business school is career jumps or career pivots. What this means is the number of changes you are making from your old career to your new one. If you previously worked in corporate finance but wanted to become an investment banker, you'd probably be able to leverage your background in finance and accounting to make a case to recruiters about your transition. But, if you previously worked as a marketer, while you could still make the transition, it would be harder to make it without the relevant or transferable skill set, or, there will be more effort involved in order to build the skills needed to get hired for that role.

While all are possible and have been done, the general rule of thumb is the more you are transitioning or pivoting, the more challenging the process will be. For example, if you are trying to change both your industry and function, it will most likely be more challenging than if you were just trying to change either of those.

Should you still choose a career even if it means you'll have to develop varied skills and engage in experiences that you don't already have? That's for you to decide. The most important point is to have a reality check on the requirements of your career aspirations.

According to Wong, "Students need to have a realistic understanding of how achievable their career goals are and how grounded they are in market demands." As an example, he said that many students want to work for Google, but Google mainly hires candidates who have professional backgrounds similar to the roles they are applying for. "If you are a student who wants to be a Product Manager at Google, but you do not have Product Management background, your chances of becoming a Product Manager at Google are not realistic." Instead, Wong suggests you consider multiple steps if this is your goal. "Students need to objectively understand how realistic their goals are compared to want they want. The best way to do this is to talk to alumni who work at the companies and in the functional areas they are interested in," Wong said.

Self-reflection as a key to identifying your career and recruiting path

Self-reflection is the exercising of introspection, coupled with the willingness to learn about yourself and what you truly want. This might mean taking the time to reflect upon what you've learned through networking or meeting with companies and take that information into account as you decide which companies or roles to apply to. For many, the recruiting and career search requires deep reflection. According to Rob Stein (Kellogg, '17), "One of the unique aspects of business school is that it is a period of time when you are forced to think deeply about your own career aspirations." While Stein was fairly certain that he wanted to pursue a career in management consulting, during his first year at Kellogg he spoke to students and alumni who pursued a similar path, internalized their lessons, and then confidently developed his own reasons for wanting to become a consultant. "I walked away much more confident about the why behind my desire to be a consultant, and how that fit in with some of my broader career aspirations," added Stein. His own self-reflection and the confidence he gained also helped in the interviewing process itself, as he was able to articulate clearly and confidently why he wanted to work in consulting, which eventually led to both a summer internship and a full-time offer.

Building your "career management" skills

While you'll be initially focused on finding the right internship, or full-time opportunity, the skills and experiences you gain from recruiting in business school are valuable for the rest of your career. They help you build the skill of "managing your career." The majority of MBA graduates will have more than one job or employer after they graduate from business school, so the ROI of developing these skills will continue to grow throughout the rest of your career. Whether that means moving up faster within your company, spotting that next emergent opportunity within your industry, or pivoting to another career avenue, learning how to take your strengths, interests, and skills and to translate them into career and job opportunities is something that you'll rely on for the rest of your career.

Jason Perocho (UNC Kenan-Flagler, '15) learned the importance of actively managing his career as a result of going through the internship and full-time career recruiting process as an MBA Student.

"The process teaches you how to identify your own goals, take in feedback from others, and build a plan for achieving those goals," said Perocho. Since graduation, Perocho has put these skills to use in his career post-business school, which has allowed him to earn three promotions in four years, and he now shares his career management approach with many of his direct reports and peers that he mentors. "Proactively managing your career is critical to continuous learning and development, which is why the internship and full-time recruiting process is valuable long after you graduate from business school," added Perocho.

Don't Forget: Aim for Your Success and Ignore the Herd!

A word of caution: Some may focus their notion of success on choosing the highest-paying career, the sexiest field, or the current flavor of the week. Many MBAs stumble into the herd mentality and end up pursuing paths that they are not really interested in, sometimes just because everyone else is doing it. It's important to remember that success is what you define it to be, not what others or society defines it as, and the quicker you can identify your own version of success, the better you can put yourself on a path towards that vision.

Consider this common scenario: You arrive on campus with clear goals for your recruitment search. The consulting firms begin recruiting and you see many of your classmates gravitating in that direction, so you join partly because you want to keep pace with the others, but also because you haven't yet gotten clear on what you'd like to recruit for. When you recruit for a position that you're not even committed to, not only do you make the process more competitive for those who are truly focused in that area, but you are less competitive due to your own lack of conviction about your aspirations. Griesser saw this frequently during her time at Fuqua, where she was surrounded by many smart and accomplished classmates. As a result, it was easy for her to feel insecure, or that she was "behind" when she saw their accomplishments or triumphs. Naturally, it was easy to compare and feel insecure.

To combat this, Griesser recommends taking time to define your own goals and values before you start the experience and to periodically ask yourself honestly how you are aligning your decisions against those goals. "I think when you are pursuing the right path for you, you get much more excited and feel much more strength and confidence in what you are doing. While I wasn't perfect with every decision, I felt so much confidence and energy with the big decisions I made, which confirmed to me I was following the values I set for myself," said Griesser.

Student Stories: Lessons From the Front Line

Each MBA student's recruiting and career path is unique. This section chronicles the recruiting experiences of several MBA students and the lessons they learned from the experience along the way.

To Find your Own Unique Career Path, Reflect and Examine

by Shannon Griesser (Fuqua, '19)

Upon graduating from Boston College with a degree in Mathematics and Theology, Shannon Griesser spent her time working in smaller organizations. She wanted to use her time at Fuqua as a means to get exposure to larger businesses within organizations and develop her soft skills. Using her own self-awareness and consistent reflection, Griesser ultimately focused her career search on corporate sustainability. Here she shares her lessons on finding her own unique path suited to her interests and her advice for managing the highs and lows of the recruiting process.

My journey to a career in sustainability

Coming into business school, I wasn't entirely clear about what I wanted to pursue for my post-MBA career, but I had a few ideas about the experiences and skills I wanted to gain. Because my professional experience was limited to small organizations, I was itching to gain some experience with a larger and more global company. Moreover, I was looking for a company with a mission-driven culture. While I had used the word "social impact" when I was coming into business school, I really didn't know how the impact was defined.

As I began attending company presentations, lunches with leaders, and coffee chats, I quickly began to learn that I really had no idea what I wanted. The field of "social impact," particularly in the for-profit world, wasn't clearly defined. I became more interested in how these large companies leverage their scale to have a social and environmental impact. Therefore, I started to focus my efforts on sustainable supply chains in large organizations.

Finding my path: trial and error

I found my own path through old-fashioned trial and error. Because I was still learning about what social impact and sustainability look like in different sectors, I quickly realized that I was not going to find my dream job or internship via the MBA recruiting process. How was I supposed to have that all figured out within the first two months of school?! I began thinking of my internship as 10 weeks of my life during which I could learn and try something new.

Coming into this process, I knew I had a lot to learn about various roles and sectors in order to understand what I really wanted. I overloaded on classes during the fall in order to take advantage of opportunities like the EDGE seminar, a weekly speaker series that brought in sustainability leaders from various companies. We got to meet with leaders from businesses like GM, Walmart, and DOW Chemical and hear how they are approaching challenges related to social and environmental impact. Finally, I focused my time on companies that had a strong, supportive culture. That became my first litmus test of whether or not I would take the time to really get to know a company and the people working there.

ABInBev had been a company that stood out from the beginning as somewhere I could envision myself working. Their presentation focused on how procurement and sustainability work in unison to achieve company sustainability goals. I participated in their case competition in the fall, which was focused on procuring renewable energy, and it exposed me to the kinds of problems I'd be solving if I was working there. They quickly became my top choice for an internship, and I was thrilled to receive an internship offer in early February.

The highs and lows of career recruiting

Like many worthwhile life experiences, there were many highs and lows. I was very impressed with how Fuqua alumni were so generous with their time. I was able to learn so much about various companies and roles through a long series of 30-minute "informational interviews" with Fuqua alumni. On the other hand, the whole process felt very inauthentic. At times, the MBA recruiting process felt like a game, and that was challenging—the condensed timeline and feeling like you were competing against your classmates for the same jobs. It created an atmosphere of anxiety and stress that you could feel for the first three quarters of your first year. Through the tough moments, there were times when I questioned my decisions or abilities, but I also always remembered that I truly believe that I'll be most successful when I define what success is for myself, but there were moments when I questioned my own abilities and tried to always remind myself of that point.

Final advice

THE RIGHT CAREER PATH ISN'T ALWAYS CLEAR-CUT

Sometimes you don't fit into a "track" like finance or marketing, and that's ok! Identify those values in a job, role, or company that matter most to you, and then chase after them.

MAKE TIME FOR REFLECTION

This should involve not only what you are good at but also what you love to do. What makes you unique? What is something that makes you light up when you talk about it? When you can identify these things, you can bring your authentic self to an interview, and that makes a huge difference.

For an MBA Career Transition, Employ a Growth Mindset

by Grace Tong (Fuqua, '19)

Grace Tong started her MBA Program at Duke University with a desire to transition into digital health. As a bioscience major, this felt like a great opportunity, but through her own reflection and research, she realized that there were some amazing opportunities to pursue within the tech sector. Employing a growth mindset and continuously reflecting and focusing on her goals paved the way for an internship and career in tech marketing.

Coming into business school, I wanted to get into digital health, an emerging field that intersects my academic background in bioscience and work experience in digital tech. However, after I got to campus, I realized that as a new field, digital health was still going through many trials and tribulations. There were limited on-campus resources for recruitment because the area is still quickly evolving. After taking some courses, I found that healthcare per se was largely subjected to public policies, and many innovations in the field were driven by tech instead. As a result, I realized that I could benefit from staying in tech longer to gain more experience. I revised my recruiting goal to management consulting firms that had a renowned tech/digital practice or big technology companies. I thought the vista point I would gain from consulting or the exposure I would get to the broader tech ecosystem from working for a technology company would allow me to continue learning in the way I desired and add greater value should I decide to pivot into digital health one day.

Since both consulting and big tech companies had structured hiring programs with my school, I mainly followed through with the on-campus resources, including workshops, training, and networking sessions put on by the career management center and career clubs.

The highs and lows of the recruiting journey

The first-year recruiting process can feel like a roller coaster ride at times because it's extremely fast-paced. Nevertheless, the recruiting process gave me some of my favorite moments in school. It was during the interview process that I met my best friends, people who share my values and who would support me through the highs and lows.

Landing the internship

By conducting my own due diligence and working alongside my peers, I was able to home in on a pitch that I thought articulated my strengths and experiences for why I was a fit for a company or role. Ultimately, I landed a role at a large technology company. To convince hiring managers that I was a good fit, I honed my problem-solving and soft skills. In my "elevator pitch," I highlighted my past experience working at the mobile gaming startup and my ability to wear many different hats and solve complex, ambiguous problems in a fluid environment.

Final advice

BE YOUR AUTHENTIC SELF

What helped me the most in the recruiting process was being my authentic self. I've learned that people are humans at the end of the day, and they want to know you for who you are. Be authentic to foster trust and treat others the way you want to be treated. It may sound cliché, but their gut feeling about whether you're likable in the first few minutes after meeting you can often override some hard, quantifiable, metrics in the recruiting process.

EMPLOY A GROWTH MINDSET

For career switchers, the ride can be bumpy sometimes. Expect to have setbacks, but never put yourself down simply because things aren't working out. Knowing that neither our intelligence nor capability is fixed and that we can always learn from our failures is key to bouncing back and obtaining personal growth.

The Joy of Thinking Deeply about your Future Career

by Mim Nothapun (Kellogg, '19)

Coming into business school at Kellogg, Mim Nonthapun knew she had an interest in the food-tech industry but was not dead set on her career path. She chose to use her time at Kellogg to think deeply about her future and what she could do to get there. Here she shares her journey and reflections from her recruiting process as well as advice for future students on how they can match their goals and circumstances to career opportunities.

Coming into Kellogg, I was not entirely set on a path for my immediate post-MBA career. I knew that in the future I would take over my family business. I had a vague idea of going into either big tech or a start-up, but my intention was to use the two years to "figure it out." So, the change I felt during recruitment didn't come as a surprise. While I had every intention of using the experience to explore, I found myself getting roped into the FOMO of recruiting for management consulting.

The rollercoaster of recruiting

The real lows of recruiting were getting rejected and seeing other people get offers before you. I couldn't help but compare myself to my classmates. I felt unqualified and doubted my own abilities. But it was a blessing in disguise. A few days later when the consulting calls came in, I realized it was not the end of the world, and Kellogg still offered me a great opportunity. Looking back, the stress came from the peer pressure and business school environment that led me to think that if I did not do as others did or if I did not have the same jobs that others did, I was not as successful.

The internship: A cold e-mail turns into an opportunity

While my initial plan didn't work out, it also gave me the chance to think deeply about what I wanted. I started the recruiting process for fast-growing startups. In addition to networking with alumni and talking to second-year students, I created a list of companies and founders that I found interesting and scoured LinkedIn and online sources for opportunities. While the effort was tedious, I began to enjoy learning about people's experiences and insights. Out of dumb luck and using LinkedIn, I found Chowbus, a food delivery startup in Chicago, and reached out to the CEO. I was fortunate that they were looking for someone in business development to figure out whether they should implement a project or not. My profile fit the bill, and I ended up interning there for the summer. Additionally, because I interned at Chowbus, I was able to secure two additional internship opportunities during my winter quarter at Kellogg. Not only did networking land me an internship, it also opened the door to more opportunities.

Final advice

PUT IN THE NETWORKING WORK

Networking can be a foreign concept, especially for students from countries where this is not a cultural norm. Even though it's not the norm, you have to learn how to do it! Take advantage of the resources the school provides. Learn from your classmates who were born in the US. Also, make sure to learn how to network efficiently. Create outreach templates, and work to identify questions that can give you insight into a company or someone's specific role.

DON'T BE AFRAID OF THE UNEXPECTED

We are all searching for something meaningful to us, and sometimes we find it in the most unlikely places. I got an internship through a cold email to a CEO on LinkedIn, which led to two subsequent internships. If I hadn't made that effort, I might not have landed any of those opportunities.

Identifying Long-term Career Goals to Jumpstart your Internship Recruiting Success

by Grant Bickwit (Darden, '19)

After spending years advising financial services companies as a management consultant, Grant Bickwit entered Darden with concrete ideas about his long-term career aspirations and identified investment banking as the path to work towards that goal. Bickwit's focus and efforts paid off, as he landed an investment banking internship, and he shared his learnings on how to successfully navigate the recruiting process.

Recruiting starts early – focus and planning help

After spending the first few years of my career advising financial services companies and banks, I decided that my plan coming into Darden was to pursue a career in investment banking.

Since the recruiting process starts relatively quickly, I made sure that I was ready to hit the ground running by identifying what I was looking for and doing my homework on the industry. This was particularly beneficial when it came time to have conversations with people during the initial round of company briefings. It was shocking to me how much richer of a conversation I could have once I showed I understood the fundamentals and how much more engaged the bankers coming to recruit were when they could talk about second- or third-level topics.

This not only helped me to stand out but also allowed me to ask better questions/get more insightful answers, which helped me to evaluate opportunities with a lot more clarity than I otherwise would have had. I was also religious about tracking my recruitment activities (events, phone calls, etc.).

While this was a pain and definitely took more time (which is in itself a precious commodity), it kept me in line and on track through the whole five months of recruitment and helped me remember the little things that turned a standard conversation into a memorable one. Furthermore, as I went through the recruiting process and began talking to recruiters, employers, and alumni, I made sure to highlight my experiences in an advisory role, especially for clients in leadership positions. While the technical/financial knowledge was important as a baseline, I learned that to truly differentiate myself as a candidate, I needed to show that I was client-ready as an advisor.

Navigating the highs and lows of investment banking recruiting

The recruiting process, especially for investment banking, is rigorous and challenging, but there are great resources at your disposal if you're willing to put in the effort. First, the network you build through the formal and informal recruiting process is incredible, and I still try to stay in touch with as many of the people I met as I can. You really are given such an incredible opportunity to learn about the career, and the access to professionals that were willing to talk to me and answer my questions was fantastic.

Obviously, juggling such a high-stakes process along with all of the other commitments and experiences business school throws at you can be challenging, but everything seems to work out of the organized chaos. It can also be pretty emotionally trying at times, as the months of hard work don't always lead to immediately recognizable results. But, the relationships I built with my classmates, who were going through it with me, helped me to navigate the challenging parts and celebrate the victories, including getting a summer internship at an investment bank.

During my summer, I felt that my internship provided me with great exposure to what a full-time role in an investment bank would be like. It was 10 weeks within one group at the bank, and over that time I was engaged in a wide variety of subject areas and responsibilities. I felt that I was as prepared as possible technically from what we had learned through our classwork, but the learning curve was particularly steep in terms of getting used to how the firm operated and all of the practical situations that an internship can throw at you.

Final advice

IDENTIFY WHAT'S IMPORTANT TO YOU

Business school is a great time to develop yourself and further your career. My advice to those who are considering an MBA is to identify what's really important for you before picking actual careers to pursue. I set a long-term career goal and identified the best path to get from where I was coming into school, and that led me to investment banking. Others in my class were more focused on other things (i.e., experiences, location). Being able to have a structured approach to filter opportunities made the exploration process much smoother during my MBA experience.

Identifying your Long-term Career Goals to Drive Short-term Success

by Winny Arindrani (Fuqua '19)

Winny Arindrani came into Fuqua with an interest to transition into the social impact space. After research, reflection, and nailing down her long-term career goals, she pivoted to pursuing and obtaining an internship in management consulting She learned how to pivot on the fly to work towards her long-term goals.

Initial plans

When I came into business school, my goal was to land a position with an investment fund dedicated to fostering social enterprises and improving financial inclusion in developing countries, especially Southeast Asia. Since I lived in Indonesia for almost my entire life, traveled to many parts of Southeast Asia, and co-founded a fashion social venture in Indonesia, I realized that financial inclusion is an important area that needs more attention from these foundations and funds.

When I arrived in Durham and started the on-campus recruitment process, I quickly realized that the recruiting process usually takes place later in the year, and most of the opportunities required further experience with financial management or management consulting, thus, I decided to pivot to recruit for management consulting roles.

While I was able to learn this somewhat quickly since consulting recruiting starts early, I was late to the recruiting process compared to some of my peers. I had to get up to speed fast, especially for interview preparation. To do this, I participated in events with the Duke MBA consulting club, especially with regard to getting up to speed on the consulting case interview process, which proved invaluable. As a part of the Consulting club, I had a first-year buddy along with a second-year mentor. These individuals helped me to practice case and behavioral interviewing to make sure I was ready for the interview. In addition to "casing," I made sure to hone the pitch that I would use with the companies. To do this, I focused on transferable skills and experiences that I felt could make me a great management consultant. As a result, I successfully landed a management consulting internship.

Success, but not without challenges

While I was successful, there were many challenging moments. I felt guilty for changing course, and I worried that by coming back to the private sector again post-MBA I would simply be "following the business school herd." I had to tell myself that it is okay to do this, especially as it is a great path to help me achieve my long-term career goals.

Final advice

LONG-TERM PLANS

For career switchers, it's important to focus on thinking about long-term plans. Most people won't work the same job forever after they graduate from business school, so you don't need to feel like you are signing up for a life sentence. If you can get a picture of what success looks like for you 5–10 years out of business school, you can focus on your time to find opportunities and experiences that can help get you to that point.

BALANCE LISTENING TO OTHERS WITH FOLLOWING YOUR UNIQUE PATH

Research and talking to second-year students and alumni are really important. Learning from their experiences, successes, and mistakes can be very valuable. However, just because they took a specific path doesn't mean you have to do the same. It's okay to not follow the herd and be different.

Hitting the Ground Running to Drive Recruiting Success

by Adam Miller (Darden, '20)

Adam Miller (Darden, '20) entered Darden with a set of career goals. But more importantly, he had a head start towards achieving them. Leading up to Darden, Miller put in extra effort to ensure that he could hit the ground running to achieve his career aspirations, and he even had time to start a podcast. In our interview, Miller shared his approach leading up to business school and how he was able to navigate his recruiting process.

I chose to attend business school because I wanted to be a Chief Human Resource Officer at a mission-driven company. To do this, I wanted to join an HR leadership development program or a human capital consulting practice in the near term. Through my research, I realized that I could go in any number of directions to achieve this long-term goal.

My recruiting journey started nine months before the MBA program started. For one, I left my corporate job in

March of 2018, which gave me plenty of time off to think about my career aspirations as well as network with lots of UVA alumni. Then, my formal recruiting process began in May, thanks in part to two programs:

1. The Consortium for Graduate Study in Management Orientation Program
2. Management Leadership for Tomorrow's Professional Development Program

Those two organizations gave me the chance to learn about consulting, brand management, and rotational leadership development programs. The summer before classes began, I had numerous interviews with various companies and even received an attractive offer. This gave me the confidence and luxury of being picky when recruiting began on campus.

The keys to recruiting success

When companies began coming to Darden in September, I went to a lot of "informational briefings" and identified 5–6 organizations I wanted to apply to.

The Bill & Melinda Gates Foundation (BMGF) was not coming to Charlottesville, but I applied off-grounds and relied on my undergrad network and the UVA undergrad network to get prepared for the interviews. I secured an offer from BMGF the day before Christmas Eve, and I immediately accepted it, meaning I had to turn down interview invitations from other firms coming to campus in January.

Final advice

THINK OUTSIDE THE BOX

There are four main industries that recruit at business school: finance, consulting, marketing, and technology. All of those are great paths, but if that's not you, don't be afraid to go off the beaten path. There are amazing firms out there that don't fall neatly into the MBA recruiting process that you should reach out to. This is not the path of least resistance, obviously, but if you realize that there's something else you'd really like to do, then go make it happen!

FIGURE OUT WHAT YOU DON'T WANT TO DO

Networking and interviewing are great ways to figure out what you want but also what you don't want. For example, I interviewed with a company who asked me what types of problems I was interested in solving. When I gave my answer, they responded with "Oh, we don't do that." Instead of feeling disappointed, I took that as a sign that the company might not be the best fit for me.

HIRING IS A TWO-WAY STREET

When it came time to find an internship, I felt excited. I came to see networking and behavioral interviewing as opportunities to share my favorite career stories and hear about what someone else loves/hates about their job. My focus was on sharing my authentic journey and asking questions that I cared about getting their feedback about.

Key Takeaways

You will spend a lot of time during your first year focusing on internship recruiting. While there will be highs and lows, it will teach you a lot that will be valuable not only for business school but also for your own learning and development for the rest of your career.

EVERYTHING IS GOING TO BE FINE!

Almost everyone gets an MBA internship during the summer, so relax; it will work out! Regardless of whether you know what you want to do or not, or if what you want changes, you will have a summer internship.

NOT KNOWING WHAT YOU WANT IS OK BUT IT REQUIRES FOCUS

Not knowing what you want, or pivoting, is perfectly normal. That said, you do have to spend time focusing on figuring it out.

IT STARTS EARLY

Recruiting starts early, especially for investment banking and consulting. Be prepared to hit the ground running.

NETWORKING IS CRITICAL TO SUCCESS

Regardless of what path you take, building relationships and networking with alumni and companies are important to the process.

USE SELF-REFLECTION AND SELF-AWARENESS

Only you can figure out what path is best for you. Take time to understand what you want and what success looks like for you, and spend time along the way reflecting on what you learn.

YOU DON'T HAVE TO GO IT ALONE

The recruiting process may seem daunting at times, but know that you are not alone. You have the second-year students, career clubs, and career management center all at your disposal to help you along the way.

Key Questions to Answer

- What does success mean for me?
- What are the potential career paths that are the most interesting?
- What skills and experiences are relevant to the career path that I'm interested in?
- What skills or experiences will I need to gain, to transition into this industry or field?
- What are the potential downsides to choosing this career path?
- Who are the people I can connect with (e.g., alumni, second-year students) who would be good to get career advice from?

CHAPTER FIVE

STUDENT CLUBS, ACTIVITIES, AND LEADERSHIP OPPORTUNITIES

Student clubs, activities, and organizations are great ways to be involved on campus, to further your career goals, and build key leadership skills

Upon entering Harvard Business School, Triston Francis (HBS, '19) had three personal development goals:

1. Build meaningful relationships with classmates;
2. Find ways to remain actively connected with HBS for a lifetime;
3. Make his mother proud.

His path towards these goals started in his first year at HBS, where he served as the education rep for his section, which is the liaison between faculty and students. This continued into his second year, where he decided to run for and was ultimately elected as student body co-president.

As the co-president, he was in charge of a 70-person team dedicated to helping improve student life for his HBS classmates. Students like Francis play an important role in the student experience. Just like at Harvard Business School, student clubs and organizations are a vibrant part of the student experience across all MBA programs. While these are great ways for students to get involved, they also serve a purpose. With aspirations for a career in management consulting and specifically leadership development, pursuing both the education rep and co-president roles gave Francis a chance to hone his leadership abilities while preparing him for his future career as a management consultant.

Clubs and organizations not only provide the campus with life and vibrancy but also give students a chance to advance their career interests, build leadership skills, and form relationships with their classmates and peers.

Types of Student Organizations

While every MBA program is different, there are three main types of student clubs and organizations:

Career and professional clubs

Typically, the most visible clubs in MBA programs are the career and professional clubs. Since many students are still exploring career options, student clubs are helpful as insights and advice regarding various industries and business functions are shared in these forums. They can help students discover the types of internships and full-time jobs that are the best fit for their ambitions and aspirations. Furthermore, joining a club with peers who have already done what you are trying to do or who are trying to do the same thing you are doing leads to learning and camaraderie. Career and professional clubs focus on career development through a number of key areas.

Diversity clubs

At Georgetown University, diversity clubs allow students to highlight and share the unique parts of themselves. For Loretta Richardson, one club that made a difference was the Black MBA Association (BMBAA). As a member of BMBAA at Georgetown, Richardson was able to get access to mentorship as well as academic and professional support to help navigate the international business world as a black woman.

Activity clubs

In addition to career-oriented clubs, many schools also have general activity clubs. Activity clubs foster growth, friendship, and networking. They create opportunities for fun as well as personal development and bring the entire community together for key events. For example, the Cocktail and Spirits Club, which hosts events around cocktail bars in Durham, organizes bar crawls through Chapel Hill and Raleigh and provides hands-on educational "classes" on how to make and enjoy classic cocktails.

SPOTLIGHT: How the Stern Women in Business (SWIB) club helps female MBA students

At NYU Stern, The Stern Women in Business (SWIB) promotes the advancement of businesswomen within and beyond the Stern community. SWIB's main focus is women's professional development, which is accomplished through a wide range of programming—from intimate fireside chats with female executives to the annual conference featuring senior leaders and Stern alumnae.

Anna Ward (NYU, Stern, '20) began engaging in SWIB events as a first-year student. She served as the Associate VP of Alumni Relations and organized an Alumni event during their Women's Week, and also spoke at another event aimed at sharing female MBA student stories with prospective students.

"Within SWIB, we try to connect with as many students as possible before they arrive, to let them know they have a supportive community waiting for them," Ward said. These groups are also great at connecting students and building relationships. During her first year, Ward also connected with a second-year within SWIB who interned at the same company Ward was going to intern at during the summer.

Now, as the co-president of the organization, Ward and her leadership team are focused on providing great resources for female students, while also engaging the larger NYU Stern community by providing space and support to discuss important issues in the workplace. For example, SWIB hosts a programming series called "Real Meals," which provides a safe, open space for discussions on tough topics and encourages students to open up, share experiences and stories, and pose any questions they might have to the group in a non-judgmental setting.

SPOTLIGHT: Participating in student clubs to further your career goals

Alexandra Jaeggi (Marshall, '20) entered business school with a desire to transition from a career in teaching to a career in marketing in the technology industry. While this meant rounding out her business acumen in the classroom, Jaeggi's engagement in various student organizations and activities gave her the skills and confidence to get up to speed on the industry and function she would be transitioning into. Furthermore, it gave her the chance to build practical skills that helped in her summer internship. "As a career switcher, engaging in opportunities with student clubs and activities gave me the confidence and skills I needed to make a career transition," Jaeggi said. As a member of numerous clubs at USC Marshall, attending events and participating in the clubs gave Jaeggi a number of key benefits.

Mentoring

As a member of the Technology Club, Jaeggi was paired with a second-year who provided guidance throughout the recruiting process." My mentor was pivotal in helping me prioritize companies, sharpen my resume and cover letter, and prepare for interviews."

Networking events

Clubs host numerous events throughout the year, to inform students about their industry or function. "These events were amazing opportunities to meet professionals with whom I could follow up and learn more independently."

Training

Throughout the year, clubs provide hands-on training to provide students with exposure to the industry. "The educational training was helpful for me to learn about the different roles I could apply for, practice casing, and learn behavioral interview techniques."

Why Participate in or Join Clubs?

At the beginning of the first year, students can sign up for club membership. Some schools have a formal process requiring paying membership dues while others are open to all who want to join. Since the clubs are student-run organizations, students also have the chance to serve in leadership positions. Second-year students serve as leaders and handle most of the big decisions and strategy, while first-year students have to apply or run for a first-year leadership position to support the second-year leaders.

MBA students have endless opportunities when they arrive on campus. So why should you get involved in student clubs and activities, either as a leader or as a club member?

Career and recruiting assistance

Getting involved in a professional or career club can further your progress when it comes to recruiting. Taking on a club leadership role can also provide you with greater access and visibility. Tony Morash (UNC Kenan-Flagler, '16) took a first-year leadership role in the Management Consulting Club. This experience allowed him to meet and engage with alumni and employees at some of the top consulting firms with which he ultimately ended up interviewing. It gave him greater insight into the firms and greater access to connections at those firms. This helped him navigate the recruiting process and land him a summer internship offer.

During her first year, Jaeggi took on an Assistant VP leadership position in the Marshall Data and Analytics Club (MDAC) and an Assistant VP for Partnerships role for MarshallWear. With both these opportunities, Jaeggi got to work on projects that helped the club execute its overall mission while enabling her to build tangible skills. For example, she developed a social media presence for the MDAC Club and a pricing strategy for the SWAG, and worked with a vendor to buy and coordinate all of the purchasing. While the tangible skills were helpful, so was the opportunity for Jaeggi to develop relationships with her peers. "In both clubs, I got the chance to build ad hoc mentoring relationships with other club leaders, who helped me navigate the first year, especially through the recruiting process," Jaeggi said.

Leadership and management skills

Many students attend business school with aspirations to attain a management or leadership position. Leadership positions in student clubs, ad hoc projects and activities offer hands-on management and leadership experience, feedback, and coaching which are invaluable to the MBA experience. From my own experience, my role as the Vice President for Diversity and Inclusion in the UNC MBA Student Association was an invaluable leadership opportunity. In this role, I was responsible for celebrating and championing diversity and inclusion through programming and student initiatives, by putting on school-wide events, championing the goals of various student groups, and working with administrators on identifying opportunities to improve the diversity of our student body. This meant collaborating with faculty, administrators and fellow students and leading events and initiatives. Furthermore, the experience and knowledge I gained have been valuable to me in my professional career as I seek to build diverse and inclusive teams. Whether it's putting into practice the cross-functional skills needed to drive a project to completion with diverse team members, or drawing on the subject matter knowledge needed to foster an inclusive team, I have relied on these learnings time and time again in my professional career.

Improving the student experience

Student organizations enrich and improve the greater community of MBA schools. Students who plan a club-run conference engage the alumni base with the school and facilitate the opportunities for students to learn and network with other professionals in their field. Students who decide to start a new initiative add new opportunities to the community. All these provide students the chance to work alongside fellow peers which often helps to form and strengthen relationships, perhaps one of the most valuable benefits of the MBA experience. These experiences are beneficial for students, the school, and the greater community.

Jasmine Ako (Yale SOM, '19) was able to make a significant impact on the lives of her fellow SOM classmates while improving her own leadership skills as a co-lead for the Yale SOM internship fund. Because of the potential to take on student debt, many MBA students choose to overlook the non-profit or social sector opportunities, but with the fund, students get a stipend that pays a competitive wage. As the co-lead, Ako was responsible for organizing multiple community-wide events and initiatives to raise money, which was then used to pay students a stipend over the summer in their non-profit internships. "It was such an enriching experience to work alongside individuals who all bought into the internship fund's mission. This experience will push me to always seek out opportunities in my career where the culture and values of the organization are aligned with my own," said Ako.

Building relationships

Working in a club or on a leadership team with other MBA students is a rewarding experience. By working alongside your peers on a big project or a tough challenge, you give yourself the chance to collaborate and get to know your classmates in a more meaningful way. Ben Thayer (UNC Kenan-Flagler, '16) held a leadership role in the Management Consulting Club and built strong relationships with many of the other officers. "Being able to throw myself into the club and helping students with a bunch of my classmates who were as equally driven and hard working as I was incredibly rewarding," noted Thayer. "To this day, they remain some of my closest friends from business school."

Regardless of what route you choose, being involved in student clubs or activities is one way to hone your own skills while pursuing a hobby, interest, or passion and acquire an

...onal experience base that will serve you for the rest of your life.

How Do you Choose the Right Clubs?

The first thing to remember is that it's impossible to do everything! You can't sign up with twenty clubs in the first week and expect to handle them all. To ensure that this doesn't happen, at some schools, clubs have membership fees to access their events or resources. You need to think about what activities will fit your goals, lifestyle, and experience. Thayer used "the rule of 3" to hone in on one activity club, one career club, and one diversity club to ensure that he focused on clubs while still making time for his other priorities. While this won't work for everyone, it's a good framework to start with.

For Bryce Parrish (UNC Kenan-Flager, '16), it was all about aligning his activities with his career interests. Parrish knew he wanted to recruit for brand management internships so he joined the Marketing club. But, he also had a passion for the Sports and Entertainment industry and knew that it was a career option he would want to potentially explore, so he joined that club too.

Matching your activities to your goals

It's also important to consider your goals and ambitions before choosing the activity that's right for you. While clubs are important, there are also case competitions, trips, and other types of experiences on campus. Students often report that the biggest benefits are being able to engage with students who share a similar interest, the chance to develop more insight into a particular field, and opportunities to network with alumni and companies that they are interested in.

Student Stories: Lessons From The Front Line

Participating in student clubs and organizations provides numerous opportunities to grow and advance your interests. These students share their experiences in various clubs and organizations and how they helped them to develop and grow.

Growing your Leadership Skills through Student Involvement

by Taylor Donner (Fuqua, '19)

Prior to attending Fuqua, Taylor Donner had a passion for serving his community, and he wanted to focus on that during his time in business school. After assessing the many options that Fuqua provided, he devoted himself fully to this goal by serving as one of the co-presidents of the Fuqua student association, which gave him ample development and growth opportunities.

Coming into business school, I wanted to take advantage of all the leadership opportunities that I could. I knew I wanted to develop while at Fuqua and thought about what positions would offer me the most transformative experience possible while still aligning with my personal interests. I have always wanted responsibility and find a lot of personal value in serving my community.

Learning on-the-fly

At the end of my first year, I was elected as one of the co-presidents of the student government association. As co-presidents, we were responsible for leading a cabinet of 11 people focused on areas ranging from academics to health and wellness. We worked together to ensure that students at Fuqua could have the best experience possible. This meant serving as a leader among my peers, working alongside students and administrators to implement new programs or initiatives, ensuring that student organizations were operating well, and listening to students and gathering feedback to relay to faculty and administrators. This experience allowed me to improve my leadership capabilities in many different ways.

First, I was able to become a more empathetic decision-maker. In my pre-MBA role, I worked for a small software development company where many of the decisions I made came from the perspective of a software developer rather than a business manager. In my role at Fuqua, I needed to take a big-picture view of how any decision we made would affect an entire community and how outcomes would be interpreted and accepted. My ability to actively seek out and empathize with the viewpoints of many different stakeholders will be essential when I become a product manager for a company that serves millions of businesses.

Second, I gained a lot of confidence in my ability to openly share my opinions in a very public forum. My role not only required me to lead meetings for a cabinet of 11 people but also communicate my viewpoints to administration and the entire student body. Before school, I worked for a very flat organization where I would express my opinions to only a few teammates and clients that I knew well. In my next position with a company of over 300,000 employees with large corporate clients, I'll be able to confidently utilize this skill set as I lead meetings and engage with senior management.

Final advice

USE BUSINESS SCHOOL TO BUILD YOUR LEADERSHIP TOOLKIT

Business school is a great time to improve your leadership expertise. Whether it's through leading student government, a club, or a team project, there are so many great projects and roles that can help you improve your leadership toolkit for when you return to the working world. Think about what skills you want to develop before you graduate, and find a position that allows you to explore your professional or personal interests.

MAKE TIME TO REFLECT

It's important to not only take on a role or opportunity but also to reflect upon what you learned after completing it. This ensures you are learning from what you are doing and improving. For example, I spent a lot of time thinking about values-driven leadership and then used my role as co-president to put those thoughts and ideas into action.

SEEK OUT FEEDBACK

One of the great things about being in an MBA program is the ability to get feedback in a safe and supportive environment, and this was especially true as MBAA co-president. Whether I wanted guidance on making a decision or needed a perspective from a fellow classmate or administrator on a specific opportunity or idea that I had, getting specific insight into what I was doing or thinking and how it could be better was critical to my learning in this role.

How to Start a Start-up (in business school)

by Colin Keeler (Wharton '19)

Colin Keeler entered Wharton with a desire to chase new career opportunities. After realizing the challenges with the MBA recruiting process, Keeler got the idea to start BeenThere, a recruiting and career platform for MBA students. Keeler shares his journey, the resources he used in business school to build his company, and the lessons he learned from the experience.

The unplanned startup

Coming into business school, I wanted to try and explore new, interesting things. Within a given career, it's easy to miss the forest for the trees, especially in industries like investment banking and private equity where I worked. At school, I knew I'd be presented with an unbelievable number of options—academic, professional, social, and more. Moreover, the extreme diversity of school necessitates a broader perspective. This was especially valuable as I considered my own entrepreneurial ambitions. Unlike some founders at school, it wasn't something I knew I was going to do for sure. I was interested in exposure to early-stage businesses, but I wasn't sure if that would mean joining a seed or series A business, venture capital, or starting my own. I considered a few ideas, but I had a real eureka moment when discussing the frustrations of career progression and business school applications. My co-founder, and now fiancée, actually had the idea as I helped her with the applications. We both said, "Wow, this is not only a good idea but could really help people otherwise stuck in a tough place." Thus, BeenThere came to be.

Building a company in business school

Today, business schools are focused on helping support and accelerate entrepreneurship. Students want more than on-campus recruiting for banking and consulting, and it really benefits schools to give them the tools to succeed. That said, it's hard. Business school is inherently a series of tradeoffs; you can't optimize. By focusing on a startup, you're diverting your time and money away from at least some of the unbelievable opportunities otherwise available. People often expect they'll come to their MBA program and be able to do it all. It's not possible. By default, focusing on BeenThere entailed diving less deeply into other areas than I might've wanted. I'm okay with that! I think the best thing people can learn is to stop managing their choices and start chasing the things that matter to them.

The MBA experience is critical to the business I've been building, so my classmates and their networks were critical in jumpstarting the business. I've also engaged with the various relevant resources on campus, including the entrepreneurship curriculum, Venture Initiation program community, and relevant clubs (Founders club, Entrepreneurship club). These have allowed me to swiftly navigate the common challenges faced by founders based on the experiences of friends and other classmates.

The learning process

Building a company in business school has been such a rewarding process. I've learned so many important lessons. First, don't be intimidated by the prospect of starting something. MBAs are often risk-averse and thus are searching for a "big enough" idea, but building a business has been one of the most rewarding things I've done, period. Second, don't underestimate the value of technical resources. Finally, plan then build. Many folks feel like they need to build what they envision as the final product immediately. This is a bad idea—your scope and needs will change, workflows will become more apparent, and you'll waste money. Get to a Minimum Viable Product (MVP) quickly and learn as much as you can.

Final advice

JUST START

If you're thinking of starting a company, just do it! Starting something is a phased process, and the sooner you start exploring it, the sooner you'll know if it's going to work. You'll find that even "menial" tasks are immensely rewarding when you're building something of your own.

MANAGE THE HIGHS AND LOWS

Starting a business is not for the faint of heart. It's hard, and there is risk involved. You need to be prepared for a roller coaster ride. It's an experience of the highest of highs and lows. Having a co-founder really helps in de-stressing the experience and thinking through options, but make sure it's the right person or it can totally derail things.

Cultivating Leadership Skills at Harvard Business School

by Triston Francis (HBS '19)

Coming into HBS, Triston Francis had big goals for accelerating his personal development, and he invested his time outside the classroom in achieving these goals. One activity that he focused his time on was serving as co-president of the HBS student association. Francis shares his goals for business school and how serving as co-president helped him build the skills for long-term career success.

A leadership learning crash course

While there was much to learn inside the classroom, serving as student body co-president at Harvard Business School was a crash course in leadership. For example, a key lesson I learned was the importance of building a team. My co-president and I decided to increase the size of our student government team by three times that of the previous board. We had a far more successful year than either of us could have imagined, and this was largely a result of us having built an incredible team. We saw our role as mainly just doing everything we could to make the lives of the people on our teams as easy as possible.

One unique aspect of serving as co-president was that I was constantly collaborating with my classmates, administrators, and professors. This was a great opportunity but also posed some unique challenges, as these are all diverse groups of people with different interests. To drive success, I would always think to myself, "How can I create a win-win-win situation?" First and foremost, I wanted to make sure that every member of my team felt as though they were getting something from being a part of student government. I wanted to help them connect what they were passionate about and their long-term goals to the student government work. This led to a win for the student leader, a win for the institution, and a win for the student body.

A chance to make an impact

Throughout the year, there were a number of projects and programs that I helped create, but the one that I am most proud of is Eat & Engage.

During my first year at HBS, my roommate and I hosted dinners at our home. As a way of breaking through the surface-level conversations of, "What did you do before school?" or, "What do you want to do after school for work?" etc., we started each dinner by reading the personal statements that we wrote when applying for admission to HBS. These were incredibly personal stories that helped get the conversations to a point of depth. It was at one of these dinners where my eventual co-president and I ended up meeting for the first time. We decided to expand these types of dinners and roll them out school-wide, resulting in thousands of interactions among students. This year at HBS, the student association launched an initiative called Eat & Engage, which is a series of subsidized small-group dinners centered around a variety of relevant issues. Each week, 6–8 students and their partners meet for dinner and thought-provoking discussion on topics from social issues to innovation to personal growth. These dinners are student-run and are hosted at a volunteer's apartment.

Final advice

TAKE ON A LEADERSHIP ROLE WITHIN YOUR MBA PROGRAM

I believe that leadership positions are an optimal way of ensuring that you make the most out of your MBA experience, and build the skills that you can use in your post-MBA career.

FOCUS YOUR "A+" EFFORT

My mentality prior to business school was, "deliver an A+ product on everything that I do." Although having a high quality of work remained important to me, I now have a mindset of, "only do the things where I am excited to deliver an A+ quality of work." I have become much more selective as it relates to where I invest my time.

TO BUILD RELATIONSHIPS, FIND PASSION PROJECTS

I think that the best way to get to know classmates is by working on a project alongside them, ideally, one in an area that he or she is passionate about. That is precisely what I got to do on a regular basis through my role as student body co-president and it led to some of the strongest friendships that I will cherish for a lifetime.

Getting Out of my Comfort Zone to Build Leadership Skills

by Reinaldo Caravellas (UNC Kenan-Flager, '19)

When Reinaldo Caravellas came to UNC Kenan-Flagler, he focused on pushing himself out of his comfort zone and tackling challenges related to his key goals. Here he shares how he was able to do this by taking leadership positions and what he learned through the experience.

Overwhelmed by so many great opportunities

After setting foot on campus at UNC Kenan-Flagler, I was thrown into so many experiences and opportunities. I focused on aligning my activities with my personal brand and goals as a guiding light. In my case, my personal brand was related to consulting, social impact, and diversity. Any time a new opportunity presented itself, I thought carefully about how well the activity aligned with my goals and personal brand/values. I did have to say no to some very tempting projects, but it was important to me to only participate in what I knew I could completely commit myself to.

One project that I worked on and am proud of is the Kenan Scholars Program for the Kenan Institute of Private Enterprise. The Kenan Institute is dedicated to "putting the private sector to work for the public good." What made this experience so valuable was the opportunity to work with well-recognized names in the diversity, inclusion, and belonging sectors, such as Dr. Jim Johnson, Lingmei Howell, and Gabriela Melo. Together, we studied the different affinity groups at UNC Kenan-Flagler and collected feedback from students, which resulted in a diversity roadmap that was fully supported by the school administration.

This project taught me how to navigate difficult conversations, engage my classmates, listen attentively, influence without formal power, and, most importantly, align the interests of major stakeholders. I have a more well-rounded perspective after this research that will serve me well in my future career. It was really important for me to understand the challenges that each minority group faces and learn from their perspectives.

Getting out of my comfort zone

I also wanted to use my time in business school to get outside of my comfort zone. I started my MBA experience by participating in a flash mob and ended it by giving a dance performance in front of 200 students. Had you told me two years ago that I would do these things, I never would have believed you! All those experiences helped me to become very comfortable in making public presentations and exploring my creative side, something that was hard for a self-proclaimed "shy guy."

Final advice

LEARN TO SAY "NO"

One of the biggest challenges for many MBA students is wanting to be able to participate in everything offered and feeling peer pressure to attend every recruiting event, social event, etc. I managed these never-ending and often competing demands by determining my personal values and goals and then filtering every opportunity through that lens.

TREAT YOUR MBA LIKE YOUR JOB

When you treat the MBA more like a job, it becomes easier to say no to some opportunities that arise, just like you would do in your career; otherwise, you would risk overcommitting and under-delivering. However, this only works when you have a well-defined strategy. If you are still deciding what to do, explore some of the events.

Building Leadership Skills by Improving Gender Equity

by Christina Chavez (Haas '19)

Christina Chavez attended Haas and planned to test out opportunities in a career in technology or strategy consulting. While she focused intensely on her career efforts, she also made time to immerse herself in numerous leadership activities, most notably in her efforts through the Gender Equity Initiative. In this interview, she shares her experience being involved in this initiative and how it helped her build her leadership skills and prepare her for the professional world.

My goal coming into business school was to start with one or two hypotheses about what I wanted to do after business school and test them out. But, outside of recruiting, I also knew that I wanted to be immersed in the Haas community. I wanted to use my time in business school to build new skills and strengthen my expertise so I could set myself up for future success following my MBA. One specific initiative that I am most proud of is my work for the Gender Equity Initiative (GEI), where I chose to focus on the gender pay gap. I worked with the Haas career management group to use data provided by alumni on their salary offers from their first job after graduating from school to analyze the gender pay gap. Using this data, my co-lead and I ran a regression of total compensation (US-based jobs only) on an indicator for gender while controlling for graduation year, industry, job function, and sponsorship status and estimated a statistically significant coefficient on gender.

The coefficient on gender estimates roughly $3.6K (based on Haas salary data from 2013 to 2018) lower total compensation for females. The statistical difference appears to be driven largely by differences in bonuses rather than in base salary. One would assume that regardless of gender, qualified men and women with the exact same education from Haas would receive equal pay for equal work. We were disappointed to discover that this was not the case even in the first year out of the MBA, with a 4% difference in pay and additional research showing that this gap only widens every year thereafter.

While conducting research, I realized that the lack of information available to women compared to men significantly contributed to the pay gap. Therefore, I convinced my team to focus on information asymmetry between genders when negotiating salaries. We created a "Haas Crowdsourced Offer and Negotiation" database that allows Haas students to share salary and bonus data openly. This helps them prepare for salary negotiations, and both men and women are on an equal playing field going into them.

To increase awareness and facilitate conversations on how and why the pay gap grows over time, we also created an infographic building on our research and other outside research on the gender pay gap. We distributed the infographic around campus, which facilitated conversations throughout our MBA class about the gender pay gap and what we could do to reduce the gap.

Overcoming challenges

Along the way, there were many critical moments and many challenges. Some challenges we faced throughout the GEI initiative involved addressing what causes the Haas gender pay gap. It is very difficult to determine causality, so we had to rely on hypotheses and outside research. Participating in GEI and many of the other extracurricular activities has helped me build leadership skills, become more resilient, and grow my relationships with my classmates. Furthermore, I have learned a lot through my extracurricular experiences at Haas about working on high performing teams and motivating others to get behind causes they are passionate about. These experiences will help me be successful in the professional world. Finally, working on these initiatives has helped me make an impact in the Haas community. Whether it was my work through the GEI or my experience mentoring underrepresented minority undergraduate students at Berkeley through the Consortium,

I feel fortunate to have made a positive impact in my time as a student leader at Haas.

How to Identify the Right Clubs to Join in your First Year

by Loretta Richardson (McDonough, '20)

With so many clubs and activities to participate in, how do you identify the right ones to select without overwhelming yourself? Loretta Richardson shares her tips.

In business school, I strive to not only learn how to grow a business but also on how to build long-lasting relationships and community. When selecting on-campus organizations, I intentionally chose clubs that would supplement the Georgetown MBA curriculum and further connect me to my MBA colleagues and the greater D.C. area. My aim was to surround myself with like-minded individuals who value service, diversity, inclusive leadership and aspire to establish a career in the same industry or function.

Joining the Black MBA Student Association (BMBAA)

I believe in the power of allyship and have always valued diversity and inclusion. According to a McKinsey & Company 2015 report, "Why diversity matters," companies in the top quartile for ethnic diversity are 35% more likely to have a financial return and 15% more likely to have a financial return with gender diversity. In short, diverse companies are more likely to achieve above-average profits. Therefore, diversity, allyship, and inclusive leadership are the requirements for successful global businesses. Being a part of BMBAA allows me to learn more about and share my culture with others and help us all prepare to be inclusive leaders. It allows us to support and encourage one another through fellowships, partnerships, and connections with alumni/leaders who share the same values.

Additional clubs and activities

What is education good for, if not to enrich the lives of others? Aside from my participation in BMBAA and other Georgetown MBA industry clubs (e.g. HoyAlytics, Tech Club), I am most proud of my participation in the non-profit Columbian consulting trek. The self-electing consulting treks at Georgetown allow us to use our business acumen to help elevate international and domestic communities. Every trek brings new challenges. How can we embrace technology, navigate a changing political climate, forge partnerships, and scale our impact? Having empathy and an international perspective are imperative to becoming a successful global leader. Hence, I always strive to lend my expertise and participate in service treks in addition to my on-campus club participation.

Final advice

FORGET WHAT LOOKS GOOD ON A RESUME

Don't get distracted by what "looks good" on a resume or what organization you can lead. Think about what type of leader you want to become. What community shares your passions? What experiences and/or skills do you need to achieve your 5-year or 10-year goals? Then narrow it down and dive-in because you do not want to spread yourself too thin.

Key Takeaways

Student clubs and activities are a critical component of the full-time MBA experience and enrich all aspects from recruiting efforts to building leadership skills. While everyone should choose the number and type of activities that are suited for them, the best way to do this is to align your activities with your own goals and priorities.

THE PULSE OF STUDENT LIFE

Student clubs and organizations are the dynamic forces of the student experience at business school. If you want to know what's going on, get involved!

FOCUS YOUR CLUBS AND ACTIVITIES

It can feel like an "all you can eat" buffet, but make sure not to get too full on clubs and activities. Prioritize and focus on the ones that align with your own goals and priorities.

LOOK FOR WAYS TO HONE YOUR LEADERSHIP SKILLS

If you're in business school, you're probably going to want to work on this at some point, and taking a leadership role in a club or organization that you care about is a great place to start.

A GREAT WAY TO BUILD RELATIONSHIPS

Participating in clubs and activities with your peers is a great way to get to know them and form bonds that will last beyond business school.

Key Questions to Answer

- Where do clubs fall within my priority list?
- What clubs (if any) are "necessary" for what I'm hoping to recruit for?
- How might a leadership opportunity in a club help me build skills or experiences?
- What other activities outside of career clubs could be a valuable learning experience?

CHAPTER SIX

MASTERING THE SUMMER INTERNSHIP

After spending a significant amount of time recruiting for an internship, MBA students head into their summer internship experience. Internships are meant to be "test drives" to further validate whether a targeted career path makes sense. To ensure that you maximize your experience and achieve your desired goals, make sure you spend time preparing for your internship.

Summer Internships

Back when I was a first-year student at UNC, in February of 2014, I signed my offer to spend the summer as a brand management intern at a CPG company. I was excited and relieved that the recruiting process was over and ready to enjoy the rest of my first year while spending some time preparing for the internship. Unfortunately, those plans went down the drain when, at the end of April, I found out that my offer was rescinded, and I needed to find a new opportunity. Fortunately, I scrambled and hustled and was able to land another internship at a dream company and in the role that I wanted. I was relieved to have found something that worked out, and I was glad to head into the summer.

While my situation is probably unique, it is reflective of the ups and downs almost every single MBA student will experience. Most schools report that anywhere between 95–99% of first-year students (who are actively looking to have a summer internship) land a summer internship, so if you are worried that you won't, the law of numbers is very much on your side!

A test drive

The MBA internship provides the ultimate hands-on experience to test drive your potential career path before graduating. It is a chance for you to get a sense of whether or not a role could be the one you were hoping to land when you first applied to business school.

Furthermore, it's a chance for you and the company to get to know each other. And, while you'll want to make a strong impression, it truly is a two-way street where you'll be evaluating the company as well. Many companies plan to extend offers to interns upon their successful completion of the internship but there are some that offer internships for the experience only. While not all students will end up working at the company that they intern for, they will gain additional experience and exposure to a role or industry.

The Internship Experience

The summer between the first and second year is the traditional internship window. While every internship is unique, there are some common characteristics.

Internships are short

MBA Internships are 10–12 weeks. This is a scant amount of time to get to know the company and to make an impact. This is especially true for internships that have fairly structured and rigorous timeframes. For example, many management consulting internships are 10 weeks long, with a mid-summer check-in coming at the five-week mark. That means you have a few weeks to prove that you are adding value and getting a good sense of whether or not you like the experience. When you are an intern, you don't have a moment to lose!

There is a lot to learn

Even with a year of business school under your belt, you will be stepping into an organization without a lot of prior knowledge. This means that you will need to invest a lot of time and energy learning your way around your new field. You'll be presented with more new information and material than you can assimilate. This is not a bad thing per se, and many people are hoping to exactly do just this—immerse themselves in a new field and learn everything about it. Even so, it can be overwhelming to have to get up to speed and learn all this new knowledge on a particular topic while simultaneously delivering a project.

You are still learning about your interests

Everyone goes in with the best of intentions to enjoy his or her summer internship. However, there is always some level of uncertainty as to whether this is the right fit. While you are expected to perform at a high level, you are also still assessing if the role, industry, or company is going to be the right fit.

From my own experience, going into my summer internship, I thought I was interested in product marketing, but I felt I needed an internship to confirm my belief. During my 12-week internship, I received exposure to various facets of product marketing, but truth be told, even after 12 weeks and a diligent effort of reflection, I truly didn't know if it was the career for me. In the end, I returned to my prior field of management consulting, but after two years, I realized that the facets of my job I enjoyed doing most tended to be most aligned with product marketing. Now, I work as a product marketer at the company where I was an MBA Intern! While 12 weeks is a great test drive, many students are still learning about themselves and their interests, and it can be difficult to feel confident in a decision either way, even with diligence and the best of intentions. If you do know, that is awesome, and you should feel confident in pursuing your goal or direction. However, if you were like me, know that it's okay! Just remember, the MBA is a degree that goes with you for the rest of your career, and the important thing is to take what you've learned from that experience, reflect on it, and use that insight to inform the future decisions that you make.

SPOTLIGHT: What lessons did MBA interns learn in their summer internship?

To better understand the experience of MBA Interns, I conducted a survey of 100 MBA students about their summer internships. Here is what they said were the most important lessons they learned from their MBA Internship:

The time flies by

"It went fast. The summer flew by and was a bit of a whirlwind. It can be easy to get caught up in the sprint of the short 10-week internship and forget to actually think about the experience and just go with the flow."

The means are as important as the ends

"It's not so much what you are proposing or finding, but the way in which you do it is critical. My findings were not that earth-shattering, but it meant delivering the message that a particular person's product was underperforming. Determining the product was underperforming was easy, but delivering the message in front of him was really hard!"

You get real responsibility

"Going in, I was a little skeptical about how much they would trust an intern with, but I ended up having an opportunity to develop their strategy for a major part of my organization's business. This made me uncomfortable, but was also the source of a lot of learning about myself and the business I was trying out."

You have to "own" your internship experience

"You have to be the master of your own destiny. If you're struggling, you need to put your hand up. If you're interested in a project or subject, you need to tell everyone who will listen. Your entire professional development comes down to your ability to be proactive and manage your own career."

Aligning stakeholders and building consensus

"If you can't work on a team, or cross-functionally, you're not going to be successful, especially in a large organization."

The importance of exceeding, not just meeting, expectations

"Doing good work is fine, but if you want to succeed you have to consistently exceed expectations. That's what helps you stand out."

Learning what you like as well as what you don't like

"I learned that I didn't actually like consulting, and during my second year, began recruiting for other functions that were more appealing.

Make Sure You're Ready to Take Advantage of the Experience!

So much effort is put into recruiting and finding the internship of your dreams! Between the career exploration process, networking, company presentations, and interview prep, you will invest a great deal of time in landing an internship. But, it is just as important to prepare for the internship as it is to land one as it will enable you to take advantage of the experience and use it to achieve your goals. (Also, this means you should probably set some goals!)

Hit the ground running

Since internships are short (10–12 weeks), make sure to hit the ground running by preparing to add value from the very first day. Brush up on your research skills from your recruiting process and get to know the company and the industry by reading articles or subscribing to newsletters. Talk to any of your classmates from the year before you who interned there last summer, or connect again with any alums at the company to set yourself up for success.

Understand expectations on (or before) day one

You should know upfront exactly how success is being defined for you—whether you achieved the organization's desired results and/or how they will determine whether or not you are getting an offer. You won't know if you're making progress toward that goal if you don't know what you're aiming for. Make sure to clarify exactly what you are expected to deliver at the end of the summer. Are you giving a presentation, producing a report, or compiling something else? Beginning with the end in mind is the best way to succeed.

Manage your summer timeline

A typical summer internship lasts between 10 and 12 weeks. Factor in the mid-internship check-in, summer vacation, and potentially a week for training and you're down to about 5–6 weeks. Keep this in mind as you map out your work plan. For example, if you have to obtain some data that you need to analyze, don't just focus on how long it takes to analyze the data; also think about how long it might take you to actually get your hands on the data. The primary mistake interns make is spending too much time with the research or not leaving enough time to practice the presentation and incorporate feedback. If you plan upfront, you will avoid these mistakes. One way to ensure you are managing your timeline is by setting some goals and working with your manager or team to ensure you are aligning towards them.

Set goals

As a Product Marketing Intern at EA Sports, Taylor O'Brien (McCombs, '17) came into his summer internship with goals to learn the subscription gaming business and learn about the role of marketing with respect to product management. He communicated these to his manager and asked for feedback, and his manager was able to ensure that he got the help he needed to achieve them. "Setting clear goals helped me focus and made sure that I was maximizing every minute of the internship experience. It also gave me a chance to go to my manager with some clear ideas of what I wanted, which helped her help me," O'Brien said.

Build relationships

Networking (everyone's favorite task in business school) is critical, and it's also a key opportunity during your summer internship. Find time on a weekly basis to have introductory meetings with alumni in the company, colleagues in different functional areas, other interns, and former summer interns. These relationships can offer you insights that can help you with your summer project, expose you to other areas of the business, and get you additional support through the summer and beyond. During his summer internship at Delta Airlines, Mark Larik (Anderson, '19) built relationships across the organization which helped him navigate his internship, and get valuable guidance for his short- and long-term career goals. In addition to relying on his manager for guidance, he found mentors whom he went to for additional guidance and feedback. "One of my mentors was in my marketing group, who taught me about the function and how to structure my project, and I had others who were not in my department but were former MBA Interns, who were invaluable for questions about career paths, culture, and general-MBA related topics," Larik said.

Proactively ask for feedback

Set up a meeting with your supervisor for guidance and feedback at least once a week. Feedback not only helps you improve your work but also demonstrates your determination to succeed. The feedback you receive can also help you discover what skills you lack to be successful in the career field. It's best to rectify these issues before you start your job and not after.

What Happens after the Internship

You've worked really hard to land the internship and focused intently on using it to help you springboard into a new career. In the end, it's an experience, and it should give you additional data points when you think about your career moving forward.

Sign on full-time

This is especially true for more established MBA recruiting pipelines, such as management consulting, investment banking, leadership development programs, and CPG brand management rotational programs. It is often at the end of the internship when they decide to make offers to interns.

Recruit during your second year

You'll have the chance to recruit again during your second year when you return to campus. Depending on your industry, timelines for this can vary, but on-campus interviewing starts in the fall.

Receiving a full-time offer is great, but it is not the be-all and end-all

The stereotypical "MBA dream" is to land a full-time offer, accept it early on in the academic year, and then have the rest of the second year of business school to pursue other interests. While that will be a true experience for some, it does not happen to everyone. In some industries, such as Management Consulting or Investment Banking, this is particularly true, as the recruiting strategy for companies in these industries is to hire full-time employees from their summer internship pool, but that is not the practice for every industry. So when you return to campus and hear about your classmates receiving job offers, it can be easy to feel bad or insecure if you don't have one, but rest assured that just because you don't have one, it doesn't mean that you are behind. And even if you do have one, it doesn't mean you have to accept it.

If you received an offer, accept it because it's what you want to do

It can be tempting to accept the offer because it's the path of least resistance, but if it's not aligned with what you want, I encourage you to reflect on your goals and interests and find an opportunity that is compatible with what you value. For example, Bryce Parrish (UNC Kenan-Flagler, '16) had a great internship experience learning brand management at a CPG company. He did receive an offer but when he went back to campus and reflected on his experience, he realized that what he really wanted was to pursue his dream in brand management—but at a sports brand. He turned the offer down and spent his entire second year recruiting for another opportunity.

If you didn't get what you wanted, know that it's okay

Nick Johnson (NYU Stern, '15) was a summer associate at a consulting firm and did not land a full-time offer. He was initially disappointed but upon reflection, he realized that the company culture and the work style of the engagement team were very important to him. This is something he came to understand as a result of his summer internship experience. Armed with these insights, Johnson landed a full-time offer at another consulting firm that matched with his goals and priorities.

If you know you won't be getting one, continue to focus on building experience

For those students who know that they won't be getting full-time offers at the end of their internship, the key here is to focus on maximizing the opportunity that they have. The industries where internship does not turn into full-time offers tend to prioritize experience above all else, so if you are in one of these fields, your job is to maximize the internship experience or parlay it into another one. Can you take on an additional project, connect with more people in the field, or ask to extend your internship experience into the school year?

Process, Not Outcomes

It is natural to believe that results (e.g., a signed offer) are measures of your success and achievements. Yes, at some point, the outcome of a full-time job is absolutely important! However, focusing solely on getting the offer is less than optimal. When you turn your attention and energy to the processes or techniques that you used during your internship, you open your eyes to more learning and will potentially be far more successful and even happier with the outcome. Overall, you gain more in life when you set your sights on the process rather than on the prize.

Finally, internships help you gain real-world experience in a particular industry or function and also give you a chance to put your skills, learnings, and experiences to work. The experience in and of itself is crucial to the launch of your career but equally important are the learnings you gained from synthesizing and assessing your internship experience which will inform your future career choices. Regardless of whether you get an offer, a critical component of the experience is taking time to evaluate what you did, and what you got out of the experience, before making a career decision.

Student Stories: Lessons From The Front Line

Preparing for your Summer Internship

by Sami Abdisubhan (NYU Stern, '20)

While Sami Abdisubhan landed his top internship choice, he knew there was more work to follow. To ensure that he was set up for success, he took advantage of the various resources on campus at NYU Stern. He wanted to make the most of his internship experience.

During my first year of business school, I was fortunate to land my top internship choice. While I was proud of this accomplishment, I knew that my work wasn't done. Whether it's to get an offer to return full-time or to show impact and success to another employer while recruiting during your second year, there's more to accomplish.

Pre-internship preparation

To ensure that I was ready for my internship, I took advantage of attending the Knowledge Management sessions put on by the Stern Graduate Marketing Association. As we got closer to the start of the summer, the sessions transitioned into how to best prepare for the job. Tips and techniques ranged from doing competitive research to chatting with consumers when shopping. I also chatted with the connections I made during the recruiting process to understand how to best navigate the organization. I visited the office a couple of times to learn about what I should expect and what I could do to prepare. Some advice I received was to take the lead on presentations to get comfortable speaking in front of large groups.

The prep helped in two ways. The Knowledge Management sessions continued to reinforce what I learned in my marketing classes and career: the foundations used for most decisions, such as the ingrained principle, "consumer first." They also, along with my coffee chats, helped me to manage expectations and to understand my responsibilities outside of the project work, such as networking within the organization, evaluating the company for my own benefit, and understanding what it means to succeed.

Internship highlights

My summer project was to revamp how my brand, Estrella Jalisco, a Mexican import in the Premium beer category, utilizes programmatic advertising, both tactically in marketing campaigns and strategically moving forward. On the creative side, I worked with our team to develop a portfolio of regional digital ads. My final deliverable was a best-practices guide full of recommendations on how to improve their utilization of programmatic marketing. My manager, brand director, had a busy summer ahead. This presented me with a challenge because he wasn't always there when I had questions or I needed input or feedback on our deliverables. I felt I needed his approval for each decision I was making, mainly because I was thinking of myself as an intern. What helped me overcome this mindset was to remind myself that my employment wasn't temporary. I reminded myself that while I was hired as an intern, a great way to show impact is to have the mentality of a full-time employee.

Final advice

KNOW THE CULTURE

A tip often shared is that one should not only come to an internship ready to work, but to be ready to network, too. It's important to evaluate the organization just as much as you're being evaluated, but I had in my head that I needed to constantly be doing coffee chats with several people in the organization, especially those who are more senior. I had a friend doing a coffee chat a day on average. Some organizational cultures are like that and some aren't, but I didn't realize that Anheuser-Busch's wasn't until I had already worried myself that I was behind. The culture is very supportive, but it's not a place where doing coffee chats for the sake of doing coffee chats is valued.

Combining Technical and Soft Skills to Master your Summer Internship

by Anne McKenna (Darden, '19)

Anne McKenna entered Darden with the goal of transitioning to a career in Investment Banking (IB). Throughout the recruiting process and internship, McKenna relied not just on her newfound accounting and finance skills but also on soft skills, such as communication and collaboration.

From education to investment banking

Prior to attending Darden, I taught eighth-grade math in a charter school and worked in private wealth management. I came to business school to switch my career to investment banking. Since I was making a change, I made sure to focus on learning the fundamentals of accounting and finance. While I'm glad I worked hard to learn these skills, I had to rely a lot on the "soft skills" that I learned from experience and my coursework. The combination of the case method and the community-like feel of Darden gave me a chance to work with others on teams and get real-time feedback. This environment was critical to helping me hone my skills, such as collaborating with others, communicating concisely and effectively, and learning new concepts quickly.

Prepping for success

Getting the internship required hard work, persistence, and effort, but I also spent time making sure that I was going to be successful during my summer. There were a number of resources that helped me prepare prior to my internship. First, Training The Street provided training sessions at Darden on the various fundamentals of financial modeling. In addition to the tactical and technical skills, our second-year students who completed Investment Banking Internships during their summers spent time with the first-year students to make sure we were educated and aware of the cultural aspects of the individual firms so that we could understand some of the nuances of the firms. Finally, our Career Development Center at Darden put on an event for all of us to understand what to expect as well as best practices for the summer.

The internship experience

The 10-week internship, while short, was fast-paced and provided many challenges. Most people in business school understand that investment banking roles require long hours in the office, but one thing I didn't plan for was what it was like to be an intern again, mostly because it had been a while since I last was one. Since the internship involves such a short amount of time, it can be a challenge to truly ingratiate yourself into the community and culture in a fast and rapid manner. Furthermore, as an intern, there is this dynamic where you sometimes are limited in the tasks you can take on or deliver because of the fact that you are new and have limited time. You're not going to transform the business overnight, so focus on other aspects where you can add value. Work hard, be open to what your team asks you to do, but be confident in communicating what you can and cannot deliver, and when you do get the chance, make sure you deliver!

Final advice

LEARN FROM YOUR ANALYSTS

In addition to being very smart and hardworking, many of the analysts have both technical capabilities as well as the ability to work fast. Many of them have been "grinding away" for two years and know a lot about how to get things done—more so than the summer associates, who are brand-new to the role. Working with them gave me the chance to learn from them as well as how to work with them, and I learned what it takes as an associate to manage them in a way that makes the best use of their aptitude and skills.

DON'T BE A JERK!

I realize that this seems very elementary, but don't be a jerk. The banking world is a small one! Be respectful of others, and don't burn bridges.

Making the Move from Start-ups to Large Companies

by Anna Ward (NYU Stern, 19)

Prior to business school, Anna Ward worked for small startups and wanted to use her MBA experience to try working for a larger tech company. After using numerous resources made available to her through NYU Stern, Ward landed a Product Management internship and got her chance to learn about working at a large tech company.

My pivot: From startups to large companies

Prior to business school, I had only worked for tiny startups and wanted the chance to work at a large technology-focused company to expand my opportunities. I wanted to understand how to add value at a big corporation, and to work within a structure where there are many levels of management above me. Previously, my bosses have always been the founders or owners of the companies I've worked for, so I focused on the tech space as I wanted an innovative environment that was hopefully more fast-paced than some older, slow-moving large organizations. In terms of functions, product management appealed to me as I wanted to own projects end to end and work with stakeholders across the organization. I ended up taking a role as a Digital Product intern at American Express, which perfectly checked all of the boxes: large organization, technology-focused, in New York City.

Using all the career resources

In order to find this opportunity, I identified someone within the Office of Career Development (OCD) during my first week who I thought would be a good ally for me. I met frequently one-on-one with that OCD contact throughout the recruiting process, sometimes to ask logistical questions and other times just to do a gut check. She gave great advice that stuck with me throughout my entire internship. One of the best experiences during my first year was the West Coast Tech Trek when we visited 14 companies over the course of five days. I was able to feel out each company in person and compare them to each other, which really helped when it came time to make decisions on my offers.

At Stern, there were other resources that helped me navigate the recruiting process.

For example, Tech in the City is an experiential learning course that pairs groups of students with startups in the city, and throughout the semester you work to solve real problems for the company. It gave me a chance to interact with executives and tackle a big-picture problem in a structured way, which was very similar to what I had to do in my summer internship. Case Competitions helped me develop structured thinking, effective collaboration within various teams, and of course, Powerpoint skills, which proved valuable during my internship.

The internship experience

During my internship, my summer project was focused on AI and machine learning. I was on the Commercial Mobile team, which manages the Amex Business App. Each team member managed a different feature of the app—working with engineers, marketing, and higher-level executives to tweak the current offerings of the app and to continue to innovate by developing and introducing new features. My recommendations focused on potential new features for the app that employ these new technologies. The project also included understanding the general competitive landscape, how other firms are using AI and machine learning and how it can most strategically be leveraged to create value for the customer and the company.

Working at a big company

My experience working at a big company was very different than what I was used to. It took me a long time to understand the org charts. Within such a large organization, it's really important to build relationships with members of a lot of different teams as you need buy-in from many people in order to move things forward. Things take longer, but they're also more thought out. I also found that within a large company we had room for a lot more big-picture thinking and future planning, whereas in my previous roles our work was much more reactionary and it was hard to find any time to plan.

Final advice

CAREER TREKS PROVIDE GREAT INSIGHT

The West Coast Tech Trek was an amazing way to connect with people at all the top tech firms and also get a feel for what they were like.

FIND ADMINISTRATORS YOU CONNECT WITH AND NURTURE THOSE RELATIONSHIPS

They will be great resources during recruiting, club management, and post-MBA.

Learning to Learn Fast and Manage Ambiguity

by Iman Nanji, (Anderson '20)

After securing a management consulting internship Iman Nanji was thrown into two separate cases with a steep learning curve. During her summer, she learned the importance of remaining confident with ambiguity in order to positively impact her team and her client.

Coming into business school, my goal was to pivot to Management Consulting, and during my summer internship, I worked at a management consulting firm in Los Angeles. During the summer, I worked on two cases. The first was a blue-sky strategy case, much like something you would see in a consulting case interview. In this case, a client asked us to help determine a go-to-market strategy for a new consumer electronics product they were launching. The second case was a personalization for a large consumer retailer. We worked on personalizing the customer journey from a digital marketing perspective.

Applying learnings from my first year of business school

During my first year of business school, there were multiple academic courses that were directly relevant to my summer internship. My strategy class was helpful for the first case and marketing was helpful for the second case. Furthermore, I also think case interview prep helped significantly. During recruiting, practicing case interviews is often seen as a necessary hurdle you have to get over to get the job, but once I actually started the internship I realized that casing is a great way to prep for thinking in a structured and comprehensive way during the internship.

Getting up to speed about consulting

One of the reasons I chose management consulting was because I like challenging assignments, and I certainly had a number of challenges to overcome. I had no familiarity with the topics for either of the cases I worked on so there was a steep learning curve and I had to work hard to get up to speed quickly.

Highs and lows

Throughout the internship, there were many highs and thankfully few lows. My highs were moments when I realized the work I was doing was really helping the team and the client. Seeing my slides making it to the client deck, presenting in meetings and answering questions others on the team had were all rewarding moments. A low moment was when we went to a client meeting and the work I had spent considerable time on was no longer relevant because the overall strategy was pivoting. While it was frustrating at the moment, in retrospect I learned a lot from doing that work even though it was no longer directly used.

Final advice

BE OK WITH AMBIGUITY

Throughout recruiting, practitioners I spoke with emphasized the importance of being comfortable with ambiguity. Over the summer, I learned how important this is. I had no familiarity with the topics for either of my cases and at first, there was a steep learning curve. It is important to approach this as a fun challenge and opportunity to learn rather than something scary or frustrating.

DON'T BE AFRAID TO ASK QUESTIONS

During internship training, we were told to ask lots of questions and try to absorb as much as possible in the first couple of weeks. So when I had questions and people were tied up I would go through all our old presentations and documents and try to learn as much about the topic as possible. By week three, everything that had once seemed foreign was making sense and I was adding value to the team in a way I didn't think was possible just a few weeks before.

Positioning myself for a Career in Product Marketing

by Ava Kavelle (Anderson, '20)

Ava Kavelle, decided to pursue a career in product marketing and landed a Product Marketing Manager (PMM) internship. During her summer, she worked on a diverse set of projects which helped her build confidence in her abilities as a Product Marketer, and a career in Marketing.

During my first year, I decided that I wanted to augment my work experience at startups by working at a large tech company. After navigating the recruiting process, I landed a Product Marketing role at a software company.

Goals for the summer internship

Going into the summer, my goals were to contribute something of impact to the team and to get experience in all aspects of product marketing. Additionally, I wanted to be a true team member, contributing something of value that my team would actually use after I left. Not only did this benefit my team, but helped my name stay in the conversation after I left!

During my summer as a Product Marketing intern, because my team was small and working on a new product, I was able to touch all the different activities and skills PMMs need to be successful: messaging and positioning, competitive analysis, customer marketing strategy, presenting and story creation, and planning events.

One of my larger projects involved running a customer webinar which highlighted how customers were using our product. This meant everything from collaborating with our sales team to figure out what type of content and audience to target, to creating compelling marketing emails and increasing registration, to developing the presentation. And of course, I presented on the webinar. If I learned nothing else, it's that everything we do as marketers all needs to lead back to performance analytics and driving revenue!

Favorite parts of the internship

I genuinely loved working on my team, being creative, and pushing my boundaries. First, my team was full of smart and kind people who are passionate about the product. It was a thrill discussing this product and industry every day and learning so much from them. Second, I love B2B marketing and having the opportunity to be creative in this type of role was fantastic. This included creating decks, writing thought leadership pieces and blog posts, developing user personas for our product and corresponding product usage stories. It was fun to incorporate a creative lens for a revenue-generating product. And lastly, really embracing the opportunity to go outside my comfort zone and do things I've never done before was rewarding. I spent most of my internship doing projects I had no experience in. Because it was such a safe environment, I wasn't afraid to put myself out there.

Final advice

KNOW THE PRODUCTS

Spend time learning the overall product suite that your company offers, and figure out where your product fits into the bigger picture. Get comfortable with speaking the language. And if you can do this before your internship starts, you'll save a lot of wasted time during onboarding!

PRESENTATIONS ARE IMPORTANT

As a Product Marketer, creating a compelling and beautiful deck, and being able to present it well, is vital. Most successful product marketers have figured out their presentation style, and are fierce presenters. As building decks and presenting are important for product marketers, I presume this is true for many other post-MBA roles, so it never hurts to brush up on your deck-building and presenting skills.

Key Takeaways

Internships are great experiences to "try for size" a new career opportunity. Just remember, while you will most likely get an internship, make sure to prepare for it and make the most of it.

EVERYONE GETS A SUMMER INTERNSHIP

Everyone lands a summer internship, so while the process can seem daunting, be confident that the numbers are on your side

DON'T FORGET TO PREPARE

So much effort is focused on landing the internship of your dreams, that people forget to prepare. Make sure you do.

HIT THE GROUND RUNNING

Internships are brief and compressed. Make sure you are doing what you can to achieve your defined goals.

PROCESS, NOT JUST OUTCOMES

It's easy to focus on the outcome, but focus instead on the process to understand what you learned, and take those insights with you as you move forward with your career after the internship finishes.

Key Questions to Answer

- What goals or aspirations do you have for your summer internship?
- What will success look like for your summer internship?
- How are you preparing for your summer internship?

CHAPTER SEVEN

SECOND-YEAR RECRUITING

While some students end up receiving full-time offers from their internships, others come back for their second year of business school to re-recruit for full-time opportunities. This is common and expected. This chapter walks through how to navigate the second-year recruiting process.

During his summer internship at a financial services company, Charlie Mangiardi (NYU Stern '17) worked on a number of highly visible projects, including the execution of a new marketing program. After making a strong impression with his final presentation, he was awarded a full-time offer. Later on in the fall, after much reflection and counsel from his peers, mentors, and career management center, Mangiardi turned down the offer and decided to enter the second-year recruiting pool. "In the end, I realized it wasn't right for my career goals," said Mangiardi.

Learning How to Recruit and Advance your Career for the Rest of your Life

Many students will go into their first year planning for and hoping that their internship becomes a full-time offer that aligns with all their MBA hopes and dreams. However, for others, there is the option of finding a full-time job during the second-year recruiting period should any of the following situations apply:

You may realize that your internship wasn't what you wanted it to be

That's great, and that's honestly part of the value in doing an internship. Now that you know it's not what you want to do, you can pursue something else. This was the case for Mangiardi, who realized that he missed the culture of a mission-driven organization and ultimately decided to pivot to something else.

Sometimes things just don't work out—it just may not have been the right fit

Things don't always go as planned, and that's okay too. Perhaps it wasn't what you thought it was. Or, maybe the role and expectations and your skills simply weren't a fit. Regardless, this is a good reason why you do an internship. It's important to reflect on the experience, but knowing that this door is now closed means that you can focus on the other opportunities ahead. Do not feel discouraged if you thought you'd landed your dream internship but then a full-time offer did not materialize. Companies that recruit on-campus understand the nature of MBA internships. While you might have to be prepared to explain your side of the story, do not be concerned that re-recruiting will be viewed as a major negative on your resume.

You always knew you'd be recruiting during your second year

You may know that going into the summer internship you will be re-recruiting during your second year. This happens for many internships that come through off-campus recruiting or with industries that typically hire just in time.

Regardless of what your reason is, developing a good game plan based on the conditions and realities of your second year is helpful in securing a full-time offer.

The Second-Year Recruiting Timeline

After coming back to school, second-year MBA students will find that recruiting starts right away. Some companies will regularly come on campus to identify students for full-time positions during the second year. Others that formally recruit on campus during the fall of the second year do so because the acceptance rate of their offers fell short of their targets. One popular field where this happens is management consulting. If your summer internship didn't work out the way you wanted it to or if you did not get internship offers the prior year and want to take another shot, this is a good time to recruit for those roles. Peter Brown (CBS, '19) recruited for full-time opportunities in October of his second year and his process for finding a role was over within the month.

For off-campus recruiting, students have the entire second year to identify their interests and to pursue them. For most students, this involves a combination of networking and exploring through discussions with other students, alumni, and companies along with some additional self-reflection and career planning with consideration to career goals and aspirations. Bryce Parrish (UNC-Kenan-Flagler, '16) decided that he was going to re-recruit in the sports entertainment industry. During the fall months, he spent time networking with alumni and building relationships with anyone in the industry so he could learn about the opportunities. As he got into the spring, he started applying for positions and leveraged the connections he made earlier in the fall.

Finally, while it's true that many students will have a job locked in right when they graduate, it's very common (and expected) for some students to graduate without employment plans. If you fall into this category, know that you are not alone. For companies that practice just-in-time hiring, your best chance to get hired happens after graduation. Regardless of why you are recruiting after graduation, it's important to ensure that you are in close contact and collaboration with your school so you can continue to take advantage of the career resources they provide. School statistics show that every year the overwhelming majority (if not all) students land a full-time job within three months of graduation.

SPOTLIGHT: Recruiting for full-time roles after your summer internships

For many students, there is an allure to land a summer internship, obtain a full-time offer, and accept the offer as you head back into your second year of business school and coast through the second year. While this is an ideal goal for many students, according to my own research conducted of MBA students this only happens for a minority of students. In a survey from August 2019, I found that 25% of students were planning on accepting a full-time offer they received from their summer internship whereas 75% of students planned on recruiting for other full-time opportunities during their second year of business school.

Within the group of students who were planning on finding another full-time opportunity, their main reason for doing so was "looking for another opportunity that was a better fit for my interests." The main takeaway here is that if you come back from your summer internship and find the need to recruit there's no need to panic. The majority of students receive job offers before they graduate from business school or shortly thereafter, and odds are that you will too.

Finding the Opportunity in your Second Year

While it's a new year, many of the same resources and practices that helped you navigate the recruiting process during your first year are still valid and important during your second year.

Network, network, network!

You need to network as much as you possibly can. More often than not, students will find their internship or job because they talked to someone who put them in touch with the right person, who then got them the position. While that may sound like a lot of work (because it is), know that most alumni and fellow students are willing to take the time to connect with you. Meet as many people as you can, and make sure your name is on the top of their minds when opportunities arise. If you are interested in an industry that uses off-campus recruiting, this is the primary way of finding opportunities.

Be open to opportunities

It is also important to be open to options that can put you in a position for success, even if the payoff will be in the longer term. An academic internship during your second year or other projects are all important because they are experiences you can add to your resume. The extra effort you make to open new doors and become more well-rounded could potentially be the reason you get the full-time offer.

Whatever happens, don't get discouraged

You may find your full-time offer early in your second year. You may find it months after your classmates. It happens. Many industries have just-in-time recruiting which means companies won't post positions until March, April, and even after graduation. So, when your classmate comes home with an offer, don't let it get you down. Stick to your plan. The key is making sure you don't give up on your search!

Student Stories: Lessons From The Front Line

Students choose to re-recruit for different reasons. Each of these students recruited during their second year.

Remaining Confident on your Recruiting Journey to Find Success

by Nick Johnson (Stern, '15)

Re-recruiting gives students another shot to find the next path on their career journey. Nick Johnson used this opportunity to reassess his priorities and identify a company and opportunity that aligned with his priorities.

The journey: From IT consulting to management consulting

Prior to business school, I came from IT consulting with the goal of going to work for a strategy or management firm, so I was initially thrilled to get an offer to join one of the "Big Three".

During my summer internship, I was assigned to a large project with a huge pharmaceutical client that was reinventing its supply model. The project had been going on for almost two years by the time I joined, and it was set to wrap in the next 3-6 months. Much of my work involved looking at all the data, decisions, and general progress to date to try and figure out how to codify what the consultants had done so the client could repeat the work.

Learning how to learn

My summer was one giant exercise in learning to learn. Although I had a consulting background, the model and structure of my former employer were different from the company that I interned at during my summer. In this project much had been done to answer the biggest questions in the first two years, a lot of what I did was figuring out what was missed and what could be done better the next go-round. I relied a lot on the project team, internal experts, and even had to embrace the full power of "Googling" it. The latter came in handy, especially when I found myself having to be self-taught on both Tableau and Excel VBA.

The reality: Sometimes things don't work out as planned, and that's okay

I did not receive an offer to return to the firm. I think by the end of the 10-week, the internship culture match wasn't what I had thought it would be during recruiting. It was disappointing, and it took a few days of time off to center myself and decide what to do next. The biggest thing is actually what you shouldn't do: panic. Yes, the summer did not go the way I thought, and it was jarring at first since I thought I landed in the perfect place to fulfill my MBA goals and post-MBA plans. What I did next was a return to the basics. What are my interests? What industry or job functions are most desirable? What career elements are non-negotiable?

After my summer, a lot of those things didn't change! What did change was my focus on people and companies that promote collaboration and teamwork. Moving forward, I wanted to use the re-recruiting process to meet people who could talk to me about day-to-day team operations. I hadn't realized it before, but the working style was far more important to me than I had known. As I went into the next round, I actually valued this element of the job search as much as things like job function, compensation, firm brand, and location.

The path forward

After assessing my interests, I kept my toe in the consulting waters, evaluating opportunities at many of the top consulting firms. I also branched out much more than in my first year. I looked at large corporate rotational management programs and internal strategy roles. One question I would often ask recruiting teams was, "Where are the biggest decisions made, and what are the challenges faced in your organization?" In this way, I felt confident that regardless of what the exact title was, I knew I would be in a fast-paced, high-impact environment.

The recruiting timeline for consulting during the second year moves fast! Time flies as an MBA in general, but I started reconnecting with my network (professors, pre-MBA colleagues, classmates, etc.) on my new search in early August, and I had my signed offer by early October. There are fewer opportunities to network in a formal setting, and you have a much better starting point in terms of interview practice.

Final advice

EVERYTHING AS AN EXPERIENCE

It's cliché and maybe even a bit corny, but everything happens for a reason. My internship didn't turn out great, but I learned a lot about what really "makes me tick" on the job—things I didn't even realize about myself. When I took that into re-recruiting, it gave me a whole different lens to look at potential firms and really helped me find a good home.

LEAN ON YOUR NETWORK

Some of my most influential conversations in re-recruiting were actually with professors. Even though they are on campus at Stern to teach and research, they've seen so many folks go through job challenges that they are a great resource for thoughts. They also get called on less than you might think for job advice, so they are super excited to spend time really thinking through your individual situation.

DON'T PANIC

You will find a job. It will take more work, but remember that you've learned a lot since your first recruiting go-round. You know a bit more about yourself and your interests, what works for you and what doesn't, what is negotiable, and what is a non-starter. Take all this additional insight and build on your long-standing MBA goals and plans—those are still valid too!

Identifying Your Goals to Drive Second Year Recruiting

by Charlie Mangiardi, Stern, '17

Charlie Mangiardi came into NYU Stern with aspirations to round out his non-profit and education experience with a more business-focused experience. After interning at a Consumer Bank and receiving an offer, Mangiardi chose to re-evaluate his career goals and turned down the offer to re-recruit for other opportunities.

Coming into business school, I wanted to round out my non-profit and educational experience by getting additional exposure in the business world. Early on, I was a bit all over the place. I hadn't come into business school with a plan or a set goal of "I want to do X when I graduate," and was unprepared for how rapidly recruiting picked up. It felt like we had to decide on a path by October. However, I was fortunate enough to get an offer for a Summer Associate position in consumer banking, where I spent my summer.

The internship experience

During my summer, I got the chance to work on new marketing technologies as a temporary project manager for a geolocation messaging pilot, while also managing several market-based microsites and working on a strategic assessment of cross-selling initiatives. Besides learning a lot about marketing, I also learned that consumer banking was not the right path for me. It was a great environment, but I missed the pace and entrepreneurial spirit of my former employer.

Second-year recruiting

After reflecting and deciding against taking my offer, I was ready to start the re-recruiting process. Learning from my first-year recruiting efforts, I took a much more discerning approach in my second year. I applied for positions at a small handful of consulting firms that allowed for an industry focus and/or limited travel; given how competitive recruiting can be for those firms, I forced myself to be comfortable with the idea of not having an offer lined up by the end of fall (since most of the types of opportunities I'd decided to prioritize didn't have formal on-campus recruiting). After a year in school and my internship, I still didn't have any greater clarity on exactly what I wanted to do after school, but I was at least much clearer on how I wanted to be doing it—in a fast-paced environment where I'd be constantly learning, and with colleagues who shared a strong sense of purpose.

The nuts and bolts of the second year recruiting process

Aside from the select few on-campus companies that met the above criteria, I really focused my attention on leveraging my network. This approach led to dozens of conversations during the fall and spring semesters, most of which was just to identify good companies that might meet the criteria. When things didn't work out with the handful of consulting firms I'd applied to in the September-October time frame, I found myself with a much longer recruitment

cycle. I ultimately got multiple offers in March and signed shortly afterward.

While the re-recruiting process was stressful, as was turning down a full-time offer, it ended up being the right decision. Being in an environment in business school where you're constantly evaluating yourself against your peers can sometimes make you feel like you need or ought to do something, but I can't stress how important it was for me to "stay true" to myself.

It can be so easy to forget the reasons you got to school in the first place. In my case, I wanted to study the intersection of finance and social impact. Once I reoriented on ways I could build on what I'd learned toward that end, it made the discernment process a lot easier. I ultimately ended up in the higher education practice at Huron Consulting Group. It was exactly the sort of work I'd wanted to be doing when I went to business school in the first place, and I'm glad I held myself accountable to my original goals.

Final advice

DON'T IGNORE RED FLAGS

I was so eager to check off some of the boxes for work, that I lost sight of some of the extremely important functional questions. For example, I completely underestimated the impact of what 80% of travel would look like for my life and state of my mind (a common story for past consultants). In retrospect, I wish I'd had much more frank and honest conversations with myself—and my wife—about the travel, and on my ability to commit to it.

NO JOB IS FOREVER

Remember that the job you're signing up for is not forever. It doesn't need to be perfect—and that's OK, so long as it's building on what you've learned and allows you to continue learning.

Building Off your First Year Recruiting Learnings

by Peter Brown (CBS, '19)

Peter Brown entered Columbia after spending his career in education to pursue a career path in technology and general management roles. His journey led him to spend the summer in an Operations Management internship, and while it was a good experience he ultimately decided to re-recruit for other opportunities. Brown shares his insights on his experience during his internship and what he learned in re-recruiting during his second year.

Switching gears: from education to technology and management consulting

As a former teacher and career switcher, I entered school with a desire to pivot to a new industry. This led me to an internship as an operations manager, where I lived and worked in southern Texas. During my summer, I had the chance to work on an exciting project, helping optimize shipping processes to improve customer experience. The most important skill I learned from this experience was data analysis. As a teacher and education professional before business school, I knew data analysis was a key area of growth for me.

Reset: Reassessing my career goals and personal priorities

After my summer internship, I decided to re-recruit for a few reasons. First, I wanted to stay in New York City after graduating from Columbia, and my opportunity would've required me to be geographically flexible. Second, I loved learning about best practices, but my long-term goals in education would've benefited more if I saw a wider range of best practices across industries and functions. I decided to recruit for consulting and corporate strategy roles at Fortune

500 companies, and I identified about 15 companies that were ideal post-MBA opportunities for my long-term goals.

Leveraging resources to identify a path forward

The first thing I did in identifying companies was to do my basic research. I wanted to make sure they met my geographic needs, that they offered long-term cross-functional opportunities, and that compensation was in line with my expectations. The second step was talking to people to get the inside scoop. My classmates who were interns were a great first source, but I also connected with at least three current employees at each company. These "culture screens" helped me figure out which of these companies were the right fit for my personality and working style. The final step was identifying the skills the companies were looking for. Sometimes I could figure this out through company presentations and coffee chats, but for a few, I reached out to my Career Management Center or the recruiter to make sure I had all the skills necessary to succeed, based on previously successful candidates at that company.

The second-year recruiting timeline is condensed and different in a lot of ways. Recruiting started once I got back to New York in late August–starting case prep, fit interview prep, and coffee chats. The nice thing is that applications were due by the end of September and interview invites came out shortly thereafter. October was full of interviews so I had to put school on the back burner for a few weeks. Luckily I got an offer from my dream consulting company at the end of October.

Differences from first-year recruiting

The main difference during my second year was the shorter time frame and the lessened emphasis on networking. By this point, I had strong relationships at every company I applied to, and it was just a matter of showing the technical skill through cases and interpersonal skills through behavioral interviews. The most important fact I learned during the re-recruiting process is how important confidence is. While I was a good caser and had strong behavioral interview prep during my first year, I was significantly more successful in my second year because I was used to the process. Instead of focusing on the exact right answer to every question, I focused on being myself.

Final advice

BE PICKY

It's easy to fall in line with the rest of the crowd, or give in to inertia and accept the first offer you get. But your second-year MBA recruiting probably offers the most access you will ever have to a huge range of well-paying, interesting, and brand name opportunities. Take advantage of this so you can set yourself up for a job that aligns with your goals.

PRACTICE, PRACTICE, PRACTICE

Practice your case and behavioral interviews with a wide range of people. It is easy to constantly practice with family and friends, but that familiarity will be very different than how you feel during an actual interview. Recent alumni and sponsored students can be a great way to learn about the company in a "safer" space, and those relationships can be vital once you start working there.

Hustling to Pursue a Career in Sports

by Bryce Parrish (UNC Kenan-Flager, '16)

Bryce Parrish had a lifelong dream, and that was to pursue a career in sports entertainment. After a successful summer in a Brand Management Internship, Parrish decided to pursue this opportunity and hustled to land a role at a leading sports company.

A summer spent at the Coca-Cola Company as a brand marketing intern between my 1st and 2nd year is an experience that I wouldn't trade for anything. Learning the fundamentals of brand marketing at such a storied brand was an incredibly worthwhile experience. Upon coming back to campus during my second year, I realized that business school was the time for me to pursue a lifelong dream of mine–landing a brand/product marketing role within the sports and entertainment industry. This decision shaped my last year by 1) forcing me to get ready for the grind of "off-campus recruiting" and 2) having to prepare for the rollercoaster of experiences this pursuit would inevitably bring along with it.

Re-recruiting for an... internship

Coming back to campus, forgoing a full-time offer, and then graduating with my classmates to pursue an internship (not a full-time offer): to be honest, at first it was scary as hell! Forgoing opportunities and bypassing the on-campus recruiting process took a ton of mental strength. Having the majority of friends either coming back with full-time offers locked down and/or landing full-time offers in early fall left me second-guessing my "roll of the dice."

But what I kept reminding myself of was that taking these two years to pursue business school at UNC was purposeful–to invest in myself and to use this opportunity as a platform/gateway to reach my end goal. Despite the rollercoaster of emotions that ensued, I had to constantly remind myself why I was there and what I needed to do to best position myself for those opportunities.

Internship round two

During the end of my second year of business school before graduating, I was able to land an internship at the dream company of mine–the Adidas Group–as an MBA Product Marketing intern on the Originals Brand Creation team.

It was an unbelievable experience working for a brand with such incredible heat and momentum behind it. Additionally, and similar to Coca-Cola, I loved learning about the heritage of the Adidas brand and the role it has played in shaping the world of sport while also creating some of the best athletes and most memorable sports moments of all time.

While I was excited about the internship opportunity, it still was nerve-wracking. I went into the internship knowing that nothing was guaranteed, so there could be a chance at the end of it that it wouldn't convert into a full-time offer. The prospect of being an MBA graduate in an internship without a path to a full-time job was daunting. But I also realized this was how it worked. The demand for roles at Adidas and companies that play in the sports and entertainment space is incredibly competitive. The approach I took to navigating that process was letting them know that I'm in this for the long-haul but more importantly, showing them–through my work and contributions–that I am deserving of a full-time opportunity if one were to present itself.

Final advice

CHASE YOUR DREAMS, EVEN IF IT'S HARD

Following your dreams is much easier said than done–it requires a relentless passion and focus to stay the course and keep pressing on, even in the hardest of times. Words can't describe how thankful I am for the opportunities I've had and how excited I am to start cranking away at the new job.

BE PROACTIVE

Recruiting for niche roles like sports entertainment requires a lot of hustle and being proactive. Continue to look for opportunities to connect with people in the industry and/or schedule in-person visits at the companies you hope to land at. *Never Eat Alone* is the name of a phenomenal book that harps on the advice above and was recommended to me by several mentors of mine in the sports industry.

How Re-recruiting During Second Year Helps Expand your Career Opportunities

by Ryan Lee, Johnson, '19

After successfully landing a summer internship in product management, and subsequently a full-time offer, Ryan Lee took a look at his priorities and ultimately turned down the full-time offer to pursue other opportunities. His second-year recruiting experience allowed him to explore additional opportunities, and land a full-time role.

Internship experience

During my first year at Cornell, after working in Financial Services, I decided to pivot my career and landed an internship at a large fiber optics company. As a Product Management Intern, my summer included a project where I worked on a long-term growth strategy to position some of the premium products. Coming from financial services, this was all new to me. I learned a lot about optical fiber from a technical standpoint, and I learned how to speak the language, which helped me gain buy-in, and most importantly, how to get that buy-in when proposing a new idea in a big forum. It was so important to talk to everyone I believed would have a question in that forum and that helped me get through my entire presentation.

I enjoyed the internship and felt I gained practical skills that would be valuable to my career. After further reflection, I ultimately decided to turn down the offer. While I liked my colleagues and I enjoyed the work, the location of the company was not somewhere that I saw myself wanting to be in the long term. Coming back into my second year at Cornell, I started the re-recruiting process and looked for additional opportunities.

Recruiting during my second year

Compared to my first year, the timeline for Product Management recruiting felt accelerated. It started the moment I returned to campus when we started talking to companies right away. In the second year, the process becomes a bit less standardized as each second year has kind of built their own network. So for some, it started even during the internship, when they realized they would not be returning. This is a reminder that while you did a lot of networking in your first year for the intention of an internship, networking really should be focused on gaining knowledge and building long-term relationships as you never know when you may need that network in the future.

While I felt more prepared for the recruiting and interviewing process during my second year, I also was almost just as busy as I was spending my time helping first-year students. At Johnson, we had a very strong culture of second-years taking on the career development role for the first-years. So allocating time appropriately was definitely the challenge. During the fall, I was fortunate to land an opportunity with a company where there was only one opening I was interested in. I knew a full-time employee who was an alum, and her guidance and insight were helpful to the process. Since she was also a recent alum who I knew well, her stamp of approval also helped expedite the recruiting process, and surely played a role in landing the offer. After interviewing from the end of November to the end of December with four companies and networking with over 20 companies, it was a relief to say that I received the offer I wanted by the end of January.

Final advice

DON'T WRITE OFF YOUR INTERNSHIP IF YOU KNOW YOU WILL RECRUIT

Make sure you know more than just your scope at your internship. Often times, I'd get asked about the other businesses at the company outside of optical fiber. And being able to talk intelligently about that helped build rapport.

EXPAND YOUR HORIZONS

There are a lot more opportunities than internships and a lot of interesting opportunities outside of the MBA traditional recruiting cycles. Sometimes it may be worth it to hold out, even if you have expiring offers, to explore what you truly want.

Key Takeaways

Students who re-recruit find their full-time opportunities throughout the entire second year and beyond. It's a normal process, and by leaning on the lessons you learned during your first year, you can achieve success.

RE-RECRUITING IS NORMAL

Many students re-recruit and choose to do so for multiple reasons.

ON-CAMPUS STARTS EARLY

Typically, on-campus recruiting starts immediately when students return from their internships. If you are planning to re-recruit for on-campus opportunities, make sure you are ready.

NETWORKING AND PERSISTENCE: KEYS TO OFF-CAMPUS RECRUITING

Since off-campus full-time opportunities can come from anywhere, networking and persistence are critical to success.

USE THE NETWORKING FOUNDATION YOU BUILT

Second-year recruiting is made easier by the network you developed from the first year of internship recruiting.

Key Questions to Answer

- What do I want to do? Have any of my aspirations changed from pre-internship? What remains the same?
- What are other roles, or functions I am interested in?
- What does the timeline for hiring for my desired track look like?

- How should I broaden my search in my second year or, on the other hand, how did the internship experience narrow my focus?
- Was there something missing in my internship that is a must-have for a full-time career?

CHAPTER EIGHT

FINAL REFLECTIONS ON BUSINESS SCHOOL

While full-time MBA programs are only two years, it can be an accelerated learning experience where students can achieve progress, growth, and even transformation in preparing for their future after business school.

If there was one word to sum up the MBA experience, it might be "journey" because it covers some time and distance but makes multiple stops along the way. Like a journey, it has a start and an end, but the distance, path, and stops along the way can sometimes be unclear, undefined, or winding.

What's so Special about Business School?

An MBA degree is often seen as an accelerator of opportunity, or a creator of mobility. And, in many ways, it is. It opens doors that were not previously there, creates opportunities that couldn't otherwise be seen, and very tactically provides benefits in the form of money and career progression, all of which can provide tangible value. But, beyond new starting salaries and signing bonuses, what makes the MBA and this journey so special?

An academic- and learning-focused environment

Academic environments are ripe for learning and learning is often a means of growth and development. Many students use the two years to accelerate their own learning, whether it's acquiring a new set of skills or gaining new experiences and knowledge. There are also some who perceive this time as a personal transformation, a shift in the mindset and thinking, a cementing of loosely held values, or a newfound sense of conviction in ideas or beliefs.

A safe space to learn, experiment, and fail

The MBA program can be a "safe place" for you to test or try out things and fail. It can be an opportunity to do something that you may not have had the desire or stomach to do previously due to fear of failure. It can also be a place where you learn to embrace activities you once feared (like reading a balance sheet). Another way to think of it is that trying and failing in your job may cost your company money, but when you try and fail in school, it's a heck of a lot cheaper. Even if failing were expensive, the value is the learning that can come with failure.

Plenty of classmates to share experiences with

One of the unique aspects of business school is the fact that you are going through a similar experience with a few hundred other like-minded people, all at the same time. Since everyone is literally and physically close to each other, this often leads to lots of opportunities to develop strong relationships and to have shared experiences. These relationships are formed through the late nights studying for a test, the trips, both formal and informal, that you may take together across the world, and through the highs and lows of preparing for interviews, late nights at the bar, and countless student activities and events.

Time to maximize your time

The reality is that there are very few times in your adult life when you have the agency to control a significant portion of your time, but business school is one of them. As an MBA student, you have the power to decide where you allocate your time. If you want to spend time focusing on academics, you can choose which classes you want to take. If you want to go all-in on building your own startup, you can put your energy there to do that.

A chance to pause and reflect

With two years to focus on development and growth, the business school also gives you a chance to breathe and reflect. Oftentimes, it can be easy to get caught up in the busyness of life, but business school gives you a chance to think deeply about what goals you want to set for yourself, to explore potential areas of development, and build a plan for how to achieve those goals. Shannon Griesser (Fuqua, '19) found her MBA experience to be a breath of fresh air: "In a world that moves so fast and with work that demands so much of our time and mental energy, business school allows you to pause and think about who you are, how you can make an impact, and who you want to be, both now, and after you graduate."

Skills that you can take with you for the rest of your career

A big focus of business school is on the skills and experiences you need to land short-term goals, such as a class, internship, or full-time job, but the beauty of immersing yourself in an MBA education is that it allows you to develop skills and lessons that you can take with you for the rest of your professional career. In the short term, that will translate into finding your next career or increasing your salary and earnings, but over the long term, your MBA education will allow you to continuously take on new roles, jobs, and careers. John Huang (Ross, '15) began his post-graduation career in an MBA Leadership Development Program at Wal-Mart. After two years, Huang grew fascinated with fast-growing startups in the technology industry and also wanted to try out marketing as a career path.

Using his experience with off-campus recruiting and positioning of transferable skills, he convinced a startup to take a chance on him and hired him for a marketing role when he had limited experience in the growth marketing space. Huang then used this experience as a stepping stone to get to Twitter for a unique marketing strategy role when he was able to leverage his Ross network to open a few doors for him. He recently left Twitter to take all of these experiences to lead growth at a fast-growing startup that focuses on supporting the careers of blue-collar workers. This all happened within the five years of his graduation from Ross. "It's fairly common to see your classmates looking for new opportunities and that helps alleviate the anxiety of switching careers until you find the right one." The good news is that what you learn in business school is applicable every time you want to make a career transition. "Business school teaches you to be curious about your career options and the value of having a network to open up doors," Huang said.

The MBA: A Force of Growth and Transformation

The following are some reasons why so many students cite the MBA program as a transformational experience. This transformation and growth occur across a number of dimensions, both in tangible and intangible ways.

Academic learning

One of the simple ways to measure the impact of the experience is to look at what you know now versus when you started, and the easiest place to look for that is within the classroom. This is an area where an MBA education can lead to significant growth, especially for students who started off without a business background. Whether it's getting a formal background in the fundamentals of business through the core classes, working on cases and projects to put learning into action, or learning from thought leaders and academics in the field, the MBA experience can increase one's knowledge base for future action. As a former marketer, Neil Zhao (Kellogg, '19) didn't have a background in finance. Taking finance classes at Kellogg opened his eyes to its importance and got him up to speed quickly. "Seeing the opportunities that come with a company having a better financial position trained me to be more comfortable with reading financial statements and understanding their impact," said Zhao.

Career growth

Students come to business school to advance their careers, and the changes students make and the doors that open to new paths are often markers of ROI and positive impact. For some, getting to their post-MBA career was not possible without making that transition. Ben Thayer (UNC Kenan-Flagler, '16) entered business school as an engineer and had never known anything else. Through his own exploration and learnings, he pivoted to a career in management consulting and took advantage of the various classes, consulting projects, and career club resources to make the transition. "In addition to exposing myself to an entirely new profession, I've also gained a perspective on my career that I never had previously," observed Thayer. His opportunities expanded greatly as a result of his MBA experience.

Leadership skills

MBA programs pride themselves on churning out the next wave of leaders and managers of the business, and while that can sometimes feel like marketing speak, students do witness changes and growth in their own personal leadership development skills. Whether it's through formal leadership positions in a club or organization, or informally learning to lead and influence through group projects or study teams, students get the chance to understand the characteristics and capabilities of good leaders and then have the opportunity to practice them. At Kellogg, Neil Zhao (Kellogg, '19) got to reflect upon, define, and grow his own personal leadership skills. By taking a class called "Personal Leadership Insights," he was able to reflect on his own unique strengths and weaknesses and craft his own leadership profile: "Prior to business school, I had management experience but hadn't thought about my own leadership style. With the class and the practice, I'm constantly trying to improve to be the best leader I can be."

One of the personal highlights from my experience was working with an executive coach. Multiple times throughout my second year of school, I met with an executive coach who provided feedback and coaching on my personal leadership style. We discussed my strengths and weaknesses, unpacked past leadership experiences to understand implications, and worked on defining my own leadership style and how I could live up to it every day. Furthermore, I had the chance to put this into practice through other channels, such as through my leadership role as the VP of diversity and inclusion in the MBA student association and other leadership opportunities.

Relationships

Having the chance to build relationships and lifelong friendships are other often-cited benefits of the MBA experience. Some happen as a result of shared experiences. Tony Morash (UNC Kenan-Flagler, '16) spent almost every day with his fellow officers in the Management Consulting Club. He formed strong relationships with these classmates, and they still take a yearly trip together. According to Morash, "When you're working alongside people every day for a few hours, you get the chance to know them, learn from them, and enjoy the experience with them." Jasmine Ako

(Yale SOM, '19) shared a similar approach during her time at Yale. While she was heavily focused on making the most of her time in the classroom, she made a point to schedule regular catch-ups with classmates that she wanted to get to know. "Those experiences, over coffee, outside of the classroom or off-campus, are what enriched my experience the most. Business school gives you the opportunity to build authentic and meaningful relationships," said Ako.

Self-awareness

As much as a business school is about developing and getting to know other people, the two-year experience is also an incredible opportunity for people to get to know themselves. For Katie Ellington (Wharton, '17), business school gave her confidence in her own narrative and awareness of the importance of sharing it. To be in business school surrounded by inspiring classmates who have accomplished so much was intimidating for her. But, as she went to class, engaged in activities, and built friendships, that all changed: "I came to see the value in my own story. Business school, for me, has been a crash course in self-discovery; your story can make the people, organizations, and community around you stronger." For many students, business school is also an opportunity to make time for introspection. "I'm much more intentional about making time for weekly or monthly checkpoints where I ask myself important questions to ensure I am going in the right direction," Tony Morash (UNC Kenan-Flagler, '16) said. "I also am much more willing to ask for feedback or guidance, whether it's from an advisor or peer, because I know their feedback can often point me in the right direction, which makes me more confident that I am working towards my goals," Morash added.

Confidence

Becoming more self-aware also enables students to develop strength and confidence in themselves and their unique talents. For Charlie Mangardi (NYU Stern, '17), gaining confidence came from learning to overcome self-doubt and imposter syndrome. Entering business school without a background in classes like finance and accounting, Mangiardi didn't always feel confident compared to some of his classmates, who had these experiences. Through time and effort, Mangiardi was able to rise to the occasion and earned an academic scholarship, but more importantly, he learned to stop questioning whether he belonged: "I learned that instead of questioning whether or not I should be there, I had to focus on pushing myself to get better."

Career development

While the focus of the MBA program is on finding the immediate career opportunity after business school, the emphasis during the MBA experience on career and personal development also helps students in their future transitions. The skills acquired from learning how to take in information, build a future path, and manage career choices are transferable and will serve the students well after graduation and throughout the rest of their careers. They will have the tools to confidently identify and take advantage of future career opportunities.

"Career development is an ongoing process you have to use regardless of the job you are in, which is why learning how to do it right in business school is important," said John Huang, (Ross, '15.) "Since the majority of students will eventually look for another job or career, learning how to set a career goal and connect your skills and experiences will make you a great candidate for a job in an interview process. Practice on how you articulate your goals will also be useful because you will need to do this for your manager so they can help you achieve them," Huang went on to add.

SPOTLIGHT: What's the most important lesson you learned in business school?

The importance of people

"The most important lesson I learned was how deeply I care about and rely on people to enrich my life. The value of the experiences I had was intricately dependent on the people with whom I shared them. Traveling the world, grinding it out in team rooms, pursuing a challenging recruiting path, were all made richer by my partner Meaghan, my classmates, professors, and the administration." - David Rokeach, Fuqua, '15

Pushing for stretch opportunities

"I took on so many 'stretch' opportunities while in business school that taught me that I never want to stop learning, pushing myself, and broadening my perspective and to stay curious and continue to grow." - Katie Ellington, Wharton '17

Honoring your interests

"I learned the importance of staying true to yourself and very intentionally following your passions and interests, which helped quell the imposter syndrome that I felt when I first started business school. The situations where I thrived the most were when I pursued electives, extracurricular activities, and career opportunities that clearly resonated with my values and just felt right." - Jasmine Ako, Yale SOM, '19

Maximizing your team

"As student body co-president, I managed a team of 70+ peers and a budget of $1.3 million. The real learning opportunity came from thinking about how to motivate peers to be excited about giving up precious time in order to give back to the HBS community. What I learned from this experience is that when building teams or coalitions, it is important for leaders to understand what those on their team want to get out of an experience. Focus on designing roles that allow people who are working with you to have a phenomenal experience, so they can get from it what they want. This way, they will be excited about what they are doing. - Triston Francis, HBS '19

Confidence in decision-making

"As a result of business school, I feel like I have a ton of power over my career, my choices, and my life path—something I don't think I had before the degree. This came from the classroom to having to make tough decisions on how to prioritize choices in business school and the confidence that if I had to pivot, or start over, I did it once and could do it again." - Kellie Braam, Booth '18

A Step on the Journey

The MBA experience flies by fast. From starting off in a new city and adjusting to a new environment to transitioning back into the working world, by the time you graduate you will have gained countless valuable experiences, opportunities, and relationships.

As rich and transformative as the experience is, remember that it is only a step on the long and even more adventurous journey of your career.

Student Stories: Lessons From The Front Line

In this section, I asked MBA graduates to reflect upon their time in business school. Their responses shed light on some of the memorable experiences, important lessons, and meaningful relationships that they've built over the past two years and paint an incredible picture of how transformational an MBA experience can be.

To make the Most of your MBA Experience, Pause and Reflect

by Shannon Griesser (Fuqua, '19)

As a career switcher, Shannon Griesser spent her time immersing herself in many experiences, connecting with as many classmates as possible, and taking advantage of all the available resources to help her transition her career. Despite how busy she was, she also made time to use the power of self-reflection and relentlessly focused on her own values to make decisions aligned with her goals and to confidently move in a direction consistent with her career that she was excited about.

A unique experience

Business school is a time where if you choose, you can take the time to try new experiences and fail without repercussion, to stretch yourself and learn your real leadership potential, and to learn from people you otherwise would have never crossed paths with. In a world that moves so fast and work that demands so much of our time and mental energy, the business school allows you to pause and think about who you are, what your strengths are, how you can make an impact, and who you want to be.

Take the time to reflect

Throughout my life, I have always tried to make space to reflect, but I made this a priority during my time at Fuqua. I was intentional about consistently reflecting and thinking through what I had done and what I had learned. One way I did this was by starting a new journal when I began my program. I wrote down my thoughts and fears and things I was grateful for. It wasn't anything profound by any means, but it allowed me to pause and reflect on the people that were making a positive (or negative) impact on my experience and to think about how I was spending my time or how I was growing. The nature of the business school is that it is so busy—socially, academically, professionally—and reflecting is not easy. So, any quiet space or a moment you can create, whether that's going for a hike on the weekend, meditating, or journaling, will make the experience that much more impactful.

Remaining confident and ignoring the herd

One of the great things about business school is that you are surrounded by a lot of intelligent, hard-working, and driven individuals. It's also a challenging thing because when you're surrounded by so many accomplished classmates, it's natural to want to step up and prove that you belong in that group. The "herd mentality" often comes alive, and it's easy to get swept up. This was something I know that I struggled with at times, as did some of my classmates at Fuqua as well as friends who were in other MBA programs. Fortunately, I was able to navigate this because I had a sense of my values and aspirations, which I defined at the beginning of the experience. Whenever I felt swayed, or even started to sway, into the herd, I'd check myself against my goals. I certainly wasn't perfect, but I think when you are pursuing the path or opportunity you really care about, you are more excited and project more confidence internally and externally than when you are trying to follow someone else's blueprint.

It's a chance to reframe your thinking

My time in business school has not only taught me things I didn't know about the business world; it also opened my mind to new ways of thinking. Most immediately, it opened doors I didn't know existed from a career standpoint. And so, as I explored those doors and listened to the career paths of successful leaders, I began to view my career as far more naturally dynamic than I had previously envisioned. Furthermore, I learned that the MBA wasn't about finding my dream job. Finding your dream job is a lifelong journey. You may be a great fit for a role or company and then outgrow it and find yourself searching for something bigger. Life might bring you to a different part of the country, and your career might come second or third on your list of priorities. The ebb and flow of a career are almost a given, and the MBA program showed me the importance of staying open-minded and continuing to build a lifelong network. The idea of a ladder you climb in your career feels incredibly outdated. While I think my career path will evolve as I evolve, the MBA gives me a lot more confidence in embracing that uncertainty.

Final advice

MAKE SPACE TO REFLECT

This is a unique time in which you have a chance to pause and reset. While you'll be doing a lot of things at any given time, make space to reflect on what you are doing so you can process all that you are taking in and learning.

SEEK OUT GUIDANCE BUT HOLD TRUE TO YOUR NORTH STAR

Your peers, classmates, professors, and administrators can teach you a lot. Seek out their counsel and advice.

However, make decisions that are aligned with your own north star, or what is best aligned to you.

Learn to enjoy the journey

The MBA is not the be all end all to a "dream career." However, it provides a great set of tools, experiences, and skills, that will help you navigate throughout your entire career, which you can use to achieve your own version of success.

Learning to Focus on What you Can Control

by Melanee Swanson (UNC Kenan Flagler, '17)

Melanee Swanson made her impact on campus by serving as president of the Management Consulting Club. Through the many experiences and her own challenges, Swanson's favorite moments were her shared experiences with others and involved the support system comprised of her family and colleagues at UNC.

My favorite moments in business school

My favorite memory of business school is not a distinct day or moment but more of a time period. Through my role as president of the Consulting Club and my work as a business communications center consultant, I spent the majority of my second-year Mod 2 and winter break helping first-year students prep for the consulting internship interview process. Watching their success in securing consulting internships made the first two weeks of January my favorite memory. I remember being glued to my phone anxiously waiting to hear from all of the first-year students. I teared up multiple times during those two weeks when I heard how amazing they were doing during interviews as well as when our Deloitte case competition team won nationals for the first time.

Looking back, I think I will miss being able to see some of my favorite people every day. Unfortunately, I had some health issues come up during my second year. But it was during that time that my friends became like family. I am convinced I wouldn't have been able to complete my second year as successfully as I did without them.

What I'm most proud of

For me, business school was a time of change and growth. The opportunities at UNC allowed me to develop into a much better leader. I took a chance during my first year and ran for the role of Consulting Club president, something I would never have done before business school. Although I had managed people in my previous job, I knew I was not a great leader and had a lot of things I needed and wanted to work on while at UNC.

When I took over the Management Consulting club, I knew that I had huge shoes to fill, as the class before us had set an extremely high bar. However, our team faced the challenge head-on, and we worked incredibly hard to make sure we didn't let down our predecessors. I have never seen so many people come together to help our classmates and our first-year students. During second-year re-recruiting, we conducted over 70 firm-specific mock interviews within two weeks, which led to an increase in second-year placement, even in a year when full-time recruiting was down. Our second-year students dedicated even more time to first-year recruiting, during which we completed over 150 firm-specific interviews in two weeks. The dedication from every consulting second-year student helped increase our international consulting placements for first-year students by 250% and our consulting placements at major firms by over 150%.

Final advice

FOCUS ON WHAT YOU CAN CONTROL

There are so many aspects of life in business school that you want to control but can't: closed lists, job offers, airport delays, group projects, health, etc. There are so many things that are pulling you in opposite directions in school that it forces you to focus only on the parts that you can control. If you worried about everything, you would no longer enjoy school, work, or life.

BUILD YOUR SUPPORT SYSTEM

The number one person who constantly has a positive influence on me is my husband. He never questioned my desire to go into consulting or my work for the Management Consulting Club, which required me to be at school practically 24/7 at times. He did everything for me in the background that allowed me to succeed. At school, my fellow classmates were also a great support system. During my first year, a second-year took me under her wing and helped me be successful both in my consulting recruiting process and in my internship. In the process, she became one of my best friends and helped me learn not to stress about things outside of my control and to enjoy every moment.

Building my Leadership Skills in Business School

by Andrés Romero (McDonough, '19)

Coming into business school, Andrés Romero understood the important role that leaders have in companies. During two years at Georgetown, his various classes, activities, and conversations with business and community leaders enriched his thinking about the roles of leaders. His time at Georgetown gave him the opportunity to develop his own leadership skills.

Memorable experiences in Washington, D.C.

After two incredible years in Washington, D.C., I walked away with many memories. But one that stood out is my Global Experience trip to Seoul, Korea, which I took during my second year. We had a global client we asked to present to while we were there. While the presentation was great, I enjoyed the opportunity to learn about the Korean culture and business environment. This was something I had no exposure to prior to business school. In many ways, this summed up a theme in my MBA experience: getting exposure to new ideas, cultures, and experiences that have enriched my thinking and mindset.

Impactful contributions

At Georgetown, all students have the skills and talents that they bring to the community each day. Throughout my time there, I made a point to use my talents to help others. One of my most important contributions was serving as a Teaching Assistant (TA) for a Managerial Statistics course because it allowed me to help my classmates who struggled with statistics. After helping some friends during my first year, I decided I wanted to apply for the TA position to support incoming first-year students. Using Instagram and slide decks with a lot of memes, I tried to make people feel more comfortable with the course content and understand it from their own experience. The immense joy I felt when people stopped me in the halls to say, "Thank you, you helped me a lot!" is something I will never forget.

A lesson in leadership

My two years at Georgetown were transformative and have made a tremendous impact on me, not only in building new skills but also in expanding my thinking and mindset. This experience changes you not only as a professional but as a person. In my case, the MBA has helped me understand leadership from a more holistic perspective. Listening to class lectures from great professors, as well as from alumni and business leaders, taught me that the world is not looking anymore for business leaders who make decisions inside closed offices, using only their judgment. I learned that this world needs leaders who can unleash the potential of their teams to serve their business and their community, and it's inspired me to work on becoming one of those leaders.

At the end of the day, businesses and companies are run by people, and people are human first. With this insight, I try to bring my own personality and passion into all my interactions. Additionally, I've also come to learn that leaders also need to take care of themselves. They need to find ways to have a healthy body and a clear mind to be able to make a more significant impact. I'm glad the program helped me to find room to address these challenges with fantastic classes, such as Meditation and Leadership or Critical Conversations, and also with invaluable experiences during the past two years.

Final advice

TAKE CARE OF YOURSELF

Mental health and self-care are as relevant—perhaps even more relevant—as any other part of your life.

PRACTICE EMPATHY

Empathy is critical in every role, at every level. We can't forget that organizations are formed by humans, and as such, personal interaction matters!

The Power of Saying "Yes" to Make the Most of the MBA Experience

by Charlotte Burnett (UNC, Kenan-Flagler, '19)

MBA students have countless opportunities to learn and grow, but doing so requires being proactive and taking action. Charlotte Burnett believes in this. Through the power of "saying yes," she has tackled many of her goals in her MBA program.

The power of yes

One of the most important lessons was, "The Power of Yes." Many people say the curse of business school is saying yes to everything; however, I would argue it is one of the best parts. Throughout my time, I said yes to a lot: case competitions, club leadership, internships, recruiting, classes, research, and the list goes on. Each opportunity was not only an opportunity to learn, but I grew professionally and personally through each experience. I am proud that when I reflect on my experience I didn't let opportunities pass me by. Go after the opportunities! You never know what will come out of them!

The highlight of my time at UNC has to be presenting our final project to Procter & Gamble Headquarters. During my first year, I was on a Student Team Achieving Results (STAR) and our team project was to analyze how P&G could increase market share in megacities. We spent the first three months researching Chinese megacities. Then, after presenting preliminary findings, we traveled to China where we conducted home visits, store visits, and meetings at P&G's Chinese headquarters. After six months of research and analysis, we presented our findings to the headquarters team. The culminating experience at the headquarters gave us the opportunity to reflect on our hard work and see the impact of our recommendations.

Building a strong business skill set

The biggest area of growth for me personally was my knowledge base about all things business. As a career switcher, I had very limited business knowledge. I knew the academics would be challenging, and I decided to use it as an opportunity. I concentrated on Investments and Capital Markets. When I reflect on my knowledge prior to business school and my knowledge now, I am amazed at how much I have grown intellectually. Furthermore, some of my growth and development came through the opportunities and activities I was involved in at UNC. I was fortunate to be involved in lots of activities. My proudest achievement from business school was the work I have done as a club leader. I served as the President of Carolina Women in Business and I am proud of the different initiatives of our club. We also hosted the largest student-run conference where we brought in guest speakers, alumni, and prospective students.

Final advice

TAKE ADVANTAGE OF THE FLEXIBILITY

You'll probably never get this much freedom with your time ever again, so take advantage of the flexibility. This is true not only in terms of your priorities but in the diversity of your activities. I love that every day is different in business school, on any day I might jump from a lecture to a team meeting and then head to a social event. I can guarantee that each day offers a new experience and opportunity.

IF YOU CAN, TRAVEL

Throughout my experience, I have also traveled to China, Hong Kong, Thailand, Indonesia, France, Belgium, and the Netherlands. Being able to do this while working full-time is not impossible but it's much more difficult. The long breaks make traveling to Asia reasonable, something I know working full-time won't afford me!

CHAPTER NINE

GRADUATION AND BEYOND

While the focus of this book has been primarily on the MBA experience, the purpose of the MBA program is to help an individual to accelerate his or her own career growth. In this chapter, we examine what comes next. What does life after business school look like? Do you actually use anything you learned in those classes? Do people end up liking their jobs? What happens if you want to change jobs?

After spending two years in Chapel Hill, North Carolina, I packed my bags, shipped them across the country and set up shop in San Francisco. I had never lived on the West Coast, and while I was returning to the management consulting industry, something I had done prior to business school, I had to re-orient back to the consulting grind, all the while adjusting to living in a new city.

In addition to all that you will learn and experience as an MBA student, you will also be preparing for the world after business school, which is another major life change. Fortunately, the skills you have developed since the onset of your studies will serve you well as you prepare to make the transition to the next leg of your journey, with your shiny new MBA in hand.

Life after Business School

After you graduate, start a new job, and resume your normal life, there are key changes and adjustments that you must make, personally and professionally. The first few weeks or months after graduation can be tough. According to Nick Johnson (NYU Stern, '15), "There were moments after

I graduated when I asked myself, 'Do I really have another 30 years of this?' Johnson continued, “The good news is that thought eventually subsides. There are so many opportunities that lie ahead of you that spending too much time reminiscing on the past only makes you miss valuable experiences. Accepting the past for what it is and giving it its due acknowledgment is fantastic. So is experiencing in the present all that life has to offer.”

New places, new people

Many graduates often end up in entirely new locations. This requires an adjustment, similar to the one that many students have to make when going to business school.

After moving to San Francisco, where I had never lived previously, I not only had to adjust to managing my job and weekly work travel but also had to actually build my personal life. Prior to business school, I lived in Boston, where I had gone to college, which meant I had friends and knew the city very well. This comfort was no longer there. As someone who thrives on relationships and community, I had to start from scratch. The challenge was attempting to do this in a new city while working at a busy and stressful job. It took me a few years, but what helped was relying on my classmates who also moved to San Francisco with me. Additionally, working at a consulting firm that also hired MBA students allowed me to form relationships with other people who were often in the same situation that I was in. These relationships with my fellow alumni and MBA graduates were critical to my settling into life after business school.

Maintaining B-school friendships

When you are in business school, you’re in a bubble, surrounded for two years by people you see every day. That environment and shared purpose give everyone the opportunity to form relationships relatively quickly. In the real world, building relationships doesn't come easily, and they take significant effort to sustain. "I was lucky to have good friends in business school who I've stayed close with many years after," said Jessi Gordon (UNC Kenan-Flager, '16). For her, taking the time to invest in and develop relationships while in business school made for a better experience then and remains valuable as she navigates her post-MBA life and career. As Gordon traveled for work, she often used this time to reconnect with classmates and friends.

Priorities are more important

In business school, time is your most valuable asset, and with a few exceptions, you have the ability to utilize your time as you see fit. While we all have some level of control in our everyday lives, unfortunately, we do not always have the ability to pick and choose the things we want to do. The business school taught you to focus on activities that align with your interests or values. According to Gordon, "Business school was a constant prioritization exercise with a lot of free time. Now, I still have to prioritize, but I have less free time!" This underscores just how important it is to understand your priorities in order to be successful.

Blending humility with confidence

Each year, thousands of people graduate from MBA programs, each eager to make an impact on the world. And, while many of them are intelligent, they have much to learn about the company or organization they just joined. You may begin your job eager to change the way your new company does things. It's important to remember that the issues you see as problems or inefficiencies are likely grounded in a tradition cultivated over time.

Jordan Nichols (Ross, '14) has seen recent MBA graduates make this mistake on a number of occasions. It is mostly well-intentioned, but it can damage your reputation right out of the gate. "Your opinion is valid, and you should express it, but this is not a peer group and there is a true hierarchy with final decision-making power landing squarely in one place," said Nichols.

You may want to demonstrate your learning and expertise right away. But, Nichols encourages students to "listen first." In many cases, there are reasons why things are the way they are. That doesn't mean they are perfect, but what it does mean is that "you should seek to understand them before trying to propose a solution."

To do this, one needs to blend both humility and confidence. Humility means being self-aware enough to know that you don't know everything. It means that you seek to listen and learn before you decide to jump in, acknowledging that there are plenty of other insightful perspectives and approaches out there. Confidence means that you believe in your abilities and skills and that you are identifying ways to put them to use. Prior to business school, Gordon was less confident in her ability to present data-driven recommendations. But, after a slew of data-intensive classes, she gained a new sense of confidence in her post-MBA career. "Now, I not only have the set of skills to do the analysis but a voice and belief in my abilities so that I can confidently share it with others."

Paths diverge

In business school, you tend to get boxed into lanes. Are you a consultant or a banker? Do you want to be in marketing or finance? Those lanes help provide focus. That structure works well in that it provides a general roadmap to hundreds of people at school, but after you graduate you begin to see that the paths diverge, and the verticals and lanes start going all over the place. Some of your classmates love what they do and hope to do it for the rest of their career, while others are already moving onto their next job.

A few months after I graduated, I remember seeing on LinkedIn that one of my classmates had already found a different job from the one he took after graduation. By the time I hit my one-year anniversary, I knew numerous classmates who had moved on to new opportunities. These are all normal occurrences. After all, it's very rare for someone to graduate from business school and spend their entire career in the same job. But, it can be easy to look around and see people making moves or decisions and wonder whether you are supposed to be doing the same thing.

It is your responsibility to find the path that is best for you, regardless of the path your former classmates are following.

SPOTLIGHT: Diverse paths after graduation

After graduation, there is no one right path to take for your career growth. The following are a few examples of MBA graduates who have taken diverse paths while pursuing their own career goals.

Growth within the same company

After graduating from UNC Kenan-Flagler, Jason Perocho (UNC-Kenan-Flager, '15) landed a Product Marketing role at a software company in San Francisco. While he has worked at the same company since he graduated, he has been promoted three times in four years, worked on four different teams, and moved from an individual contributor position to a people manager role. "I've enjoyed working for the same company, but have always found plenty of new exciting challenges and opportunities within my company," Perocho said. Perocho credits his success to being proactive and working for supportive managers and leaders. "I believe that everyone should take ownership of their career, and am very proactive and vocal about what I want to achieve. But having managers and leaders who develop their people has been a critical part of my ability to get those roles and experiences that I've had in my time so far," Perocho said.

Growth in new industries, functions, and companies

Prior to business school, John Huang (Ross, '15) worked as a management consultant, where career paths were very well defined. "The career ladder was very straightforward. If you wanted to be promoted, you had clear metrics to hit," Huang said. While this served Huang well as he navigated the consulting firm, his post-MBA career had gone in a different direction as he started discovering the type of work he enjoyed doing the most.

Finding a career that he was passionate about came from a long process of elimination. It started with working on projects across a dozen Fortune 500 companies in multiple industries as a consultant and exploring experiences with startups and starting his own business while at business school. Since graduating from Ross, Huang continued to search for the right fit for his skills and passion going from the world's largest company with over 2.2 million employees to a startup with only 10 employees.

His career path had taken him through Finance, Strategy and Operations, and Growth Marketing and after three companies in four years, he found his dream job as the director of community and growth at a fast-growing startup with an incredible mission to serve blue-collar workers.

"I would have never predicted landing where I am today in a million years nor could I have guessed all the steps I had taken to get here. However, by being comfortable with risk and consistently listening to my internal feedback to guide my career goals, I was able to build confidence and narrow down my definition of a fulfilling career without ever knowing the exact next step," said Huang.

Putting your MBA to Work for your Career

The lessons you learn, the people you meet, and the growth you enjoy during your MBA experience will be with you for the rest of your life. So, how will your life be different as the result of obtaining an MBA?

A network of peers

"The strong network of peers and allies you've cultivated will continue to be there for you. Sarah Rumbaugh (Darden, '15) founded RelishCareers while she was a student, and since then she has called on her classmates and fellow Darden alumni numerous times as she's built her company. Over the years, she's relied on this network to create business contacts, identify customers, find partners, and so much more.

Lifelong career development

If you're like most MBA graduates, the first job you take after business school won't be your last; you'll have to look for a new job at some point. For your entire career, you will benefit from the career development and recruiting lessons that you acquired in business school. These skills were relevant for Gordon, who after 3 years of HR consulting post-graduation, decided to make a transition to business development in the Healthcare industry. When Gordon realized it was time to look for a new opportunity, she relied on the career development toolkit she built in business school to identify the next steps for her job search. Gordon stated, "I always tell people that the process we went through to get our internships is foundational for the rest of our lives. The networking, coffees, phone calls, awkward cold emails—all of these will happen again."

Confidence in decision making

During your MBA experience, you're constantly given the chance to make decisions. While this can be overwhelming, it also helps students develop confidence in cementing priorities and values, as well as coming up with a sound process for making decisions. "During business school, I had so many choices. Learning how to make tough decisions gave me confidence that I know how to make a decision that's aligned to my goals, and that even if I make a wrong decision, I'll be OK," said Kellie Braam, (Booth, '18) Now, Braam feels empowered as she navigates her career post-business school. "While I may not know exactly what the rest of my career and life looks like, I have the confidence that I can use what I learned in business school to make career and life decisions that are aligned with my goals," said Braam.

Navigating the gray

Partly through experience and wisdom and partly through business school, Ashley Wells (Wharton, '16) has become more adept at navigating the "gray" areas of life: "I used to be more comfortable with black and white, but after navigating so many ambiguous situations in business school, I've begun to understand that life is much more gray." This can be daunting or challenging, especially for people who are accomplishment driven and want to succeed at a definitive goal or metric. However, graduates like Wells have learned to embrace the ambiguity and gray, and to use the skills they learned in business school to navigate the opportunities and challenges that come up in life.

Throughout my own life, I have always prided myself on having a plan. Winston Churchill's "failing to plan is planning to fail" resonated with me, and I also made a point of being proactive about my own goals and aspirations along with creating tactical steps and action plans to help me get to where I plan to go. For the most part, that has worked out very well. In high school, my goal was to get into a good college, and upon graduating from college, my goal was to move into a good career and position myself to go to a good business school. After graduating from UNC, I had finally done all those things, and I was left with the question, "Now what?" At first, I will admit, I had a bit of fear because I didn't have a concrete plan for what was next. But, I've become more adept at navigating in those gray spaces without an exact or clear plan, and instead, relying on my skills and experiences to work through ambiguity. I can attribute this partially to my time in business school, where I had the chance to confirm and solidify many of my key values and aspirations. So, with confidence in what I've learned about exploring ideas, an approach to career development, and a much stronger network, I believe that, while I may not have the right decision at any given moment, I have the resources to figure it out.

The Journey Continues

The MBA experience is an important experience, but it is one of many on a lifelong journey. As the MBA graduates in this chapter have mentioned, while there are many challenges ahead, they also present opportunities to put your learnings to use. Life after business school gives graduates a chance to put what they have learned into practice and to apply the skills and tools they learned in business school, allowing them to make meaningful contributions throughout the rest of their journey.

STUDENT STORIES: LESSONS FROM THE FRONT LINE

What is life like after business school? I asked a number of MBA graduates to share what their transition back to the professional world was like, how they navigated their journey since graduating, and how they used what they learned in business school to help them along the way.

To Learn and Grow After Business School, Stay Curious

by Ashley Wells (Wharton, '16)

After graduating from the University of Pennsylvania, Ashley Wells moved across the country to San Francisco and started her post-MBA journey. While there have been unexpected turns along the way, Wells' desire to stay curious and take risks has led her to unexpected but meaningful opportunities, and here she shares how this impacted her life after business school.

Going back to the working world is like getting back on a bicycle—except that during your time off the bike, you've been lifting weights a lot, so you're ready to come back faster and stronger. In case this metaphor isn't landing, what I mean is that essentially the day-to-day logistics of being back to work (five days per week!) were exhausting at first and then quickly became normal. What was more interesting is that I felt I grasped business concepts much quicker than pre-business school, and I felt that my business acumen and hard and soft skills were much more robust. I knew enough to be "dangerous" in nearly any section of the business that I worked in thanks to my Business school coursework, and I felt ready to manage people and teams due to the strong emphasis Wharton placed on management, negotiations, empathy, leadership, teamwork, and building diverse and inclusive teams.

One of the biggest things business school taught me was not to fear uncertainty as well as to have confidence in myself to take risks, knowing that change is inevitable and healthy. It would be really boring to know exactly what I will be doing in 5, 15, or 30 years, and the uncertainty is now exciting, whereas when I was 25 I was anxious to have all the answers about my purpose in life. Paraphrasing writer/thinker Liz Gilbert, in life there are woodpeckers (who have a singular purpose that they chip away at relentlessly) and hummingbirds (who go from branch to branch pollinating as they go to make the world more beautiful over time in a non-linear fashion), and I'm finally satisfied and proud to be a self-proclaimed hummingbird.

Expect a bit of the unexpected

Just shy of two years of being back in consulting (which was my pre-MBA background), a previous client reconnected with me to recruit me for a full-time role working for them. Initially, I didn't take the opportunity seriously. First, I needed to finish my two-year commitment to my employer, and second, I had mentally set expectations that I'd undergo a serious career search at the two-year mark to discover all my options. Though the possibility caught me off guard, I began to see the absolutely incredible opportunity for what it was—a chance to help run a business transformation that I had designed, in a role that I could customize and build, under the best leadership I'd ever worked with, which I knew would inspire me and help pull me up in the company if I worked hard. My role at Adobe far surpassed any box I could have hoped to check, and I had the added benefit of knowing what I was getting into based on my past client experience. It was unexpected, but I took a leap of faith in myself. I love my job, and it feels amazing to say—and believe—that.

Putting your MBA to work

The MBA is a critical period of time, but what it does for your life moving forward is just as important. My MBA gave me professional confidence in my business acumen and leadership potential and a deeper curiosity to view and solve problems through nuanced angles. Pre-B school I was more comfortable with "black and white" choices and decisions, but I've learned how much work (and real life) is about navigating the gray. Personally, I was lucky to meet some of my closest friends, who are all going to run the world's leading companies and organizations someday, and there's no price you can put on calling those friends up when you need them for their counsel and friendship.

To make your MBA work for you, start by thinking of the ways that you surprised yourself in B-school. Did you enjoy a class you never thought you would? Dance on a stage in front of hundreds of people? Travel to a country previously off your radar? Learn about new career paths that piqued your interest or changed your trajectory? Many of the ways you surprised yourself were because you allowed yourself to take risks in what you perceived as a "risk-free" environment. Now that you're in the real world, ask yourself, how many choices can you truly make that are irreversible? The answer is very few. This means that real life offers you every opportunity to surprise yourself and take chances just as you did in B-school, which is a huge mental freedom.

Final advice

GIVE BACK

Help others going through the process as you were helped, and give back to current students.

MAKE TRADITIONS

Make traditions and keep them—for example, all of us who were part of an MBA leadership group take time to write the group a letter every day each summer. That means 40 letters filled with meaningful updates on friends' lives, even though we don't get to Facetime all that often. Finally, apply yourself; if you're not applying at least 80% of your brain and talents week to week, do yourself (and the world) a favor and go find somewhere else where you can contribute more meaningfully. Stay curious.

Leveraging your MBA Network to Grow your Career

by Sarah Rumbaugh (Darden, '15)

As the founder of a recruiting and talent startup, Sarah Rumbaugh knows the importance of building a great network—it's one of the reasons she chose to attend Darden, and that has helped her scale RelishCareers over the past few years. Here she shares with us how her MBA has helped her grow her business and the valuable lessons she has learned.

Life after business school

There are lots of reasons why life after business school is great, but one of the most exciting things was having an income again! This was a bit different for me though because I was starting my own business, and I actually spent the first handful of months without paying myself. Nonetheless, it was exciting when I started to pay for myself!

I also enjoyed not having to study for and take exams. In a lot of ways, transitioning back into the working world was something to look forward to for me because I started my business while I was still in school, so I was doing both (school and work) before graduating. One thing that I certainly missed after graduating was the tremendous amount of human energy and intellect that exists in business school (i.e., you're surrounded by your classmates in business school).

When you're in the throes of business school, there can seem like a lot of worries. For example, I worried about doing well on exams and finding the "right way" to answer academic questions, but I've learned since business school that focuses on individual strengths, working with others who are complementary, being comfortable with the unknown, and actually seeking opportunity from the unknown can get you far in life.

I learned a lot in business school, but one of the most important things is that there's never enough time in the day for everything you want to do, at least in regard to work stuff. Business school helped me learn to prioritize the most important things on a given day as well as realize that work/career is less about finding the "right answer" and more about finding the "right way to think about and execute" work/career activities.

In terms of the unexpected, well, I'm engaged to my business cofounder and our COO! We've learned a lot about how to work together and how to separate the business from other parts of our lives—family, friends, hobbies, etc.

In terms of how the MBA continues to help my career, the network it provides continues to pay dividends for me. The difficulty of the education and work-life balance it provided continues to help me be at ease and still grow in difficult life challenges.

Final advice

LEVERAGE YOUR NETWORK

Take advantage of the relationships with classmates, friends, professors, alumni, recruiters, career services—it is a great way to grow your career for many years to come. I used this network to create business contacts, customers, partners, etc. While leaving business school can be a bummer, life after business school can be really great. There is so much to look forward to.

DO A "LIFE" AUDIT

First, write down, literally write down, your career and life aspirations. Connect how they all fit together. How do your career aspirations fit with your life aspirations in general? Do they make sense together? Don't modify them if they don't seem to fit together, but ask yourself how you can make them fit. When you write this down, tell yourself that you don't have to show it to ANYONE. This way, you'll be as honest with yourself as you can be regarding what truly matters to you. Then, when you're making actual career decisions (i.e., when you're applying to jobs, interviewing, getting offers, getting rejections, etc.), remember what you wrote down—and remember it as you continue to make career decisions year after year. What you wrote down doesn't need to be based in reality. It doesn't even need to be an aspiration that you feel is realistic. It simply needs to be something that you really, really want because, when you're making actual career decisions, you do need to think through how your decisions impact many aspects of your life. So, if you make decisions that feel like a compromise, you'll understand why. Over time, you'll learn how to incorporate what you truly aspire to into a world that makes sense for you.

Raising your Hand and Focusing on the Present

by Jessi Gordon (UNC, Kenan-Flagler, 2016)

After graduation, Jessi Gordon moved to Washington, D.C., traveled weekly on airplanes, bought a new home, and watched friends come and go. Through her post-grad life, Gordon has relied on her knowledge and experiences from business school to become a better problem-solver, to be more comfortable with data, and to cultivate her confidence to pursue her aspirations.

The transition to the real world

In my experience, there are two pieces of the transition that can be tough: the social aspect and the routine. On the social front, I consider myself lucky because so many of my classmates joined me in D.C., so I've been able to stay connected to some of my closest friends. I did struggle with the travel requirements for my new job, though. As I tried to build my life in D.C., I found it hard to make plans and establish myself because I traveled every week. For the first year, I felt more like I lived in California than in Washington, D.C.

Learning and growing after business school

I graduated from Kenan-Flagler in 2016 and moved to Washington, D.C. The Trump presidency and subsequent #MeToo movement have, of course, been catalysts for change across the board. I have personally changed my perspective on workplace culture. I used to think that having women and people of color in leadership roles was an indication of inclusive culture; I've come to realize that companies must prioritize and support this diversity to be inclusive. That said, culture is hard to assess as an outsider. But if you do your due diligence (more than just reading Glassdoor.com) and have some less formal conversations, you should be able to get a better sense of a company's inner workings. In my most recent job search, I talked to eight people outside of the formal interview process to get a good handle on the culture around inclusiveness at my current company.

In my career, I've become an infinitely more confident problem solver—and more skilled at it, too. Business school (and my policy program) provided me with the tools to advise on everything from entering a new market and developing revenue projections to performing valuations and learning the regulatory environment.

I have been able to put my data skills to use as well, synthesizing information into concise findings and recommendations. Before business school, I found myself nervous about providing recommendations and insights to clients and internal stakeholders. Post-UNC, I not only have the skill set to produce this work, but I can remind myself that I am likely the person in the room most familiar with the data, which provides a confidence boost I can feel great about.

The benefit of hindsight

Knowing what I know now, I would have worried less. I'll confess—I'm a worrier! I worried a lot about the future. I worried about my internship and my full-time job. I worried that I wasn't enjoying my time enough. I did take advantage of being back in school because I love learning. I took the opportunity to take classes that were challenging and on topics that I knew absolutely nothing about. But still, I wish I'd cherished every problem set a little more.

I have a few friends from various stages of my life who have since gone to business school or are currently enrolled, and I've noticed the same patterns. We're all so focused on the future! That's probably a key driver to attend business school in the first place. But with the benefit of hindsight, I do wish I'd realized how fleeting my time would be, and I wish I'd taken the time to focus a bit more on the present.

The value of the MBA from here

I always tell people that the process we went through to get our internships is foundational for the rest of our lives. The networking, coffee shop meetings, phone calls, awkward cold emails—all of these will happen again. And when they do, you'll need to rely on your networks—educational, professional, and personal—to help you take your next step. It's also helpful that people know what an MBA means—it's a very versatile degree with a high labor market value. In my most recent job search, I was interviewing for roles that felt above my weight class (try to avoid that impostor syndrome!), but I think they appreciated that I have my MBA.

Final advice

RAISE YOUR HAND

Get in front of people. If you're interested in a project, tell someone. If you want to learn something, speak up. You can always bring a different perspective, and if you refuse to accept the status quo, you will figure out how to provide value.

ALWAYS KEEP YOUR EYES OPEN

You never know what opportunity might be around the corner. It's easy to stay in a job if you're comfortable, or if you feel some sense of loyalty to the people who hired you. Comfort and loyalty can be great! But it's also important to have consistent check-ins with yourself to determine if you're happy, challenged, and fulfilled in your career.

APPLY TO ONE NEW JOB A YEAR

Apply whether or not you actually want to leave. You can at least feel confident that you know what's out there. At the very least, it's great for practice and for gaining new insights about your field, your prospects and, most importantly, yourself.

The Little and Big Lessons for MBA Graduates

by Jordan Nichols (Ross, '14)

After graduating from Ross, Jordan Nichols moved to San Francisco and began a career in tech, working with larger tech companies and smaller startups. Through these experiences, he's learned lessons along the way that have helped him chart his career post-business school.

The little things

While there is work in business school, there is also the understanding that the ultimate goal is graduation and landing a quality job once that day comes. Discipline, perseverance, and fortitude will propel candidates forward in their careers as they perform their duties day-in-day-out. However, in an MBA program, there are only a few tests, quizzes, projects, and deliverables per course. This means you are not graded on your performance on a regular basis. In an MBA program, you have the luxury of keeping up with the work and then hunkering down when it is time to get to business.

A lesson I wish I had learned earlier in my career is that while being smart is a nice leg up, and while being educated and having an MBA will give you access and opportunities you otherwise might not have, being reliable and consistent is the most important trait of any employee or partner. This is how you will prove you are an invaluable asset to your team.

The big things

You have a boss. This means that not all opinions are equal, and that, generally, you are not entering into a leadership role. This is the most acute reality I have seen my peers struggle with coming back into the workforce. You must learn to defer to your boss. You just spent two years working in groups with only peers. Sometimes you elect a group leader. However, their superiority is granted by group consensus, and there is nothing to stop any member from bucking their leadership outside a poor peer review. Along with this, you just graduated from a top MBA program and have been told the world is yours for the taking. You have been stuffed with more frameworks and problem-solving techniques than you can count. You have an answer to every question and case studies to reference.

Listen first

However, the reality is that wherever you land, you have a lot to learn. The problems and inefficiencies you see with the current order of business at your new company or in your new role likely have logic or rationale behind them that has been learned and implemented through years of experience. Your opinion is valid and you should express it, but this is not a peer group and there is a true hierarchy. Final decision-making power lands squarely in one place. There will be an inherent urge to flex all the muscles you have worked on for the past two years and prove to your team that you are worth the six-figure salary and signing bonus you have just been granted. You want to question everything, rewrite the processes that seem inefficient, and show everyone they made the right decision. If there is one piece of advice I can give for your first three months on the job it is this: Observe, ask questions, and listen.

Final advice

AVOID FEAR OF JUDGEMENT (FOJ)

Business school is the time for FOMO (Fear of Missing Out) to the max. However, I believe FOJ (Fear of Judgement) is really the more apt term for what drives many people's decisions during and just after business school. I have known sales was the best direction to take in my career for quite some time. However, once I got to business school I realized sales was not one of the prestigious careers my classmates and alumni respected. I would be lying if I said it never got to me. We all desire the respect and admiration of our peer group, especially in this environment. As I have gotten older, and as I have progressed in my career and become more secure in my own value and skill-set, my anxiety about how others perceive me has turned to pride.

Learning to Adapt to Find New Career Opportunities

by Nathan Tanner (Marriott, '15)

Nathan Tanner started his career in Investment Banking and used his time in business school to pivot to a career in HR. After graduating from BYU, he started in an HR role at a large tech company and has since transitioned to a hypergrowth tech startup. Tanner's ability to adapt has enabled him to learn quickly and take advantage of career opportunities that are aligned to his interests and aspirations.

Post MBA graduation goals

Coming out of business school, I had two primary goals. The first was to find a job and career path where I could leverage my strengths. I thought that would be HR but wasn't totally sure. The second goal was to achieve the first one without sacrificing what's most important in my life, specifically, my family and my faith. I definitely achieved my first goal as I feel really confident that I'm on the right career path. I definitely had some doubts during my first year after school but things have really solidified in the years since. As for the second goal, I've done an adequate job. Some times I've been better at focusing on family and faith than at other times, but for the most part I've been able to keep things in perspective. Overall, I feel good about my progress toward both goals.

Overcoming unexpected challenges

I worked for LinkedIn part-time during my second year of B-school. When I joined full-time, I quickly learned that the skills needed to be successful in my new role were drastically different than anticipated. I took this pretty hard. I was in a funk for a month or so as I felt more confused about the future of my career than when I had started grad school.

My initial urge was to go find another job. I confided in a trusted colleague and he helped me see things from a different perspective. He helped me understand that even if I didn't want to stay in that role long term, I had a unique opportunity to develop skills that would help me in future positions. I had open conversations with my manager about my long-term plans which influenced the types of projects I worked on. Speaking up allowed me to identify projects that were more interesting and leveraged my strengths.

Several months later I transferred internally to a role that was a better fit, but there were two big lessons that came from that experience. First, I learned that you can change your job without actually leaving it, and second, I learned that we all have more power than we think we do.

A mindset shift that leads to personal success

I felt some angst during and right after business school. Far too often I used my classmates as a benchmark when I should have focused on how I was progressing. As time passed and I've found a career path that I'm happy with, I'm less focused on comparisons and I'm not constantly trying to figure out what to do next. I enjoy what I do on a daily basis.

Business school gave me the tools I needed to make a pretty drastic career change. The relationships I made, both with professors and with peers, have been invaluable. I acquired several mentors along the way who have helped me see the world from a different perspective. I certainly learned a lot from my courses, but I believe I learned even more from the people I met along the way.

With this in mind, a few years ago an opportunity came up in my career to try something new and different, which involved transitioning from a large company (10,000+ employees) to a hypergrowth startup. Leaving LinkedIn to join DoorDash was a tough decision and the first few months were incredibly challenging. DoorDash was 250 employees and I was initially tasked with leading our HR team. Our headcount has grown almost 8x since then and my role has changed several times. We've grown really quickly and I've had to learn a lot on the fly. There's been a lot of growing pains along the way but I'm proud that I've been able to keep going.

Final advice

EMBRACE UNCERTAINTY WITH AGILITY

In the conclusion of *Not Your Parents' Workplace*, I shared that those who will be most successful in their careers will be those best able to adapt. It's fairly easy to put that on paper. It's a lot harder going through the challenges that come from adaptation.

Key Takeaways

The learning and growth from your MBA experience don't stop when it ends. After you graduate, your journey continues, and the MBA provides you with the skills and experiences to make the most of the journey ahead.

RELATIONSHIPS MATTER

The relationships you build with your classmates matter after graduation. These relationships can be beneficial as you adjust to a new city or new career or simply to help you when you're looking to make a career move yourself.

PATHS DIVERGE

People go in different directions and at different speeds and that's okay. The important thing is to move in the direction and at the pace that makes sense for you.

OWNING YOUR DECISIONS

Making a decision means acknowledging you won't be selecting alternatives. While that can create FOMO, it can also be empowering. Selecting decisions that are right for you, and focusing on your own path can be very freeing.

THE JOURNEY CONTINUES

Business school doesn't take away the uncertainty, but it does help you sort through it. There will be unexpected things that happen throughout the rest of your life, but the skills and experiences you learn can help you navigate those, personally and professionally.

Key Questions to Answer

- What have you learned since you graduated?
- How have you grown since you graduated?

- How much closer to your goals are you since you graduated?
- Where do you hope to be in 5-10 years?

AFTERWORD

Did you Leave it All Out There?

Growing up, my favorite sport was basketball, and I started playing basketball when I was six years old. From around the ages of 8-12, my father was the coach of my team, and as the coach's son, in addition to getting the same guidance and coaching that the rest of my teammates received, I always got the "director's extended cut" before and after games, and even at points in between.

Fortunately, amidst all the commands and guidance my father gave, there were many that were on point. One of his favorites that he consistently said to me and our team was, "Did you leave it all out there?" This meant, at the end of each game, win or lose, could you walk away knowing that you gave your all on the basketball court, or did you come up short in some way, shape, or form? This lesson fueled my preparation and work ethic for the game.

While that analogy of "leaving it on the court" is what I used to motivate myself to run wind sprints, shoot foul shots, or dive for a loose ball before it went out of bounds, it may also serve as a metaphor for how you think of your time in business school. When you are there, are you doing all that you can to make the most of your experience? Are you taking advantage of as many resources that your school offers to you to enhance your career? Are you taking the time to build relationships with your peers, classmates, and administrators? And are you taking advantage of all the things that you won't get to do when you leave and head back to the working world?

I remember graduation after an incredible two years at UNC, and walking across the stage and picking up my diploma. While there were many reasons to be sad (going back to work after two fun years seemed like the last thing I wanted to do…), I felt a sense of pride and contentedness because during my time in business school I felt that I had made the most of my time while I was there. I took advantage of every class I wanted to take, formed great friendships and relationships with classmates and professors, furthered my own career development and made an impact on the greater community through involvement in various student clubs and organizations. In short, I had made the most of my MBA experience.

My hope for you is that after reading this book, you have both the strategic guidance and the tactical next steps to do the same. Every student has a path and journey but by delving inside the MBA experience, you have the insight, tips, and thought frameworks to go build your path to success.

Now the question becomes, "Will you go out there and leave it all on the court?

ACKNOWLEDGEMENTS

During Christmas break in December 2018, I made a goal that I would focus in 2019 on the things in my life that are important to me, that align with my values, and that give me energy. As the dust settled, one of my resolutions was to write a book. Well, here we are! This has been a fun and challenging journey with lots of learnings, but at each step along the journey, I've had an incredible support system that guided me to make this a reality.

MOM, DAD, AND ERIN

For always being my biggest supporters, for encouraging me to be the best version of myself, and for inspiring me to live what you have taught me. I enjoyed this project because it encapsulates so many elements of who I am, which all of you are responsible for shaping. Thank you for your unconditional love, support, and inspiration.

MY EXTENDED FAMILY

For always supporting me and encouraging me to pursue big dreams, and for being my biggest cheerleaders. Also, thank you for continuing to believe that I look younger every time I see you.

MEGHAN GOSK

You were the first person I seriously pitched this idea to, and your immediate response of, "You have to do it!" was the affirmation I needed to get started. I'm grateful for your support, mentorship and guidance, and for sharing similar values and beliefs that are rooted in the communities that we've both been influenced by.

JON FARBER, KIRSTEN SMITH, JEFF CHEN, JESSI GORDON, COURTNEY WRIGHT AND TONY MORASH

Your feedback, edits, ideas, and corrections of grammar, syntax and spelling (even when I told you that you didn't have to) are the reason this book got finished. Thank you for your willingness to help, and for your friendship.

UNION STREET ROASTERY

Thank you for allowing me to set up shop on weekends and for the great coffee that fueled this book.

THE TEACHERS, ADMINISTRATORS, AND EDUCATORS FROM MCQUAID JESUIT HIGH SCHOOL, BOSTON COLLEGE, AND UNC-CHAPEL HILL

Thank you for the work you do in educating and empowering people to learn and grow. Your work is important and has influenced my own love for learning.

WITH GRATITUDE

I am a big believer in the power of stories, and in particular personal and human stories. We all want to connect and identify with others, which is why I've gone out to listen to hundreds of stories from MBA students, and have showcased some of them in this book. If you find any or all of these stories to be helpful or valuable and that they resonate with you, it's because of the people below. Though I am indebted to hundreds of people, I want to thank the many students and graduates here who graced the pages in this book, in alphabetical order:

1. Sami Abdisubhan (NYU Stern, '20)
2. Jasmine Ako (Yale SOM, '19)
3. Winny Arindrani (Fuqua, '19)
4. Grant Bickwit (Darden, '19)
5. Kellie Braam, (Booth, '18)
6. Peter Brown (Columbia Business School, '19)
7. Charlotte Burnett (UNC Kenan-Flagler, '19)
8. Reinaldo Caravellas (UNC Kenan-Flagler, '19)
9. Christina Chavez (UC Berkeley-Haas, '19)
10. Taylor Donner (Fuqua, '19)
11. Jeff Ellington (Wharton, '17)
12. Katie Ellington (Wharton, '17)
13. Andi Frkovich (LBS, '21)
14. Triston Francis (HBS, '19)
15. Jessi Gordon (UNC Kenan-Flagler, '16)
16. Shannon Griesser (Fuqua, '19)
17. John Huang (Ross ,'15)
18. Alexandra Jaeggi (Marshall, '20)
19. Ava Kavelle (Anderson, '20)
20. Najee Johnson (UNC Kenan-Flagler, '15)
21. Nick Johnson (NYU Stern, '15)
22. Nate Jones (McCombs, '19)
23. Nishanth Kadiyala (UNC Kenan-Flagler, '16)

24. Maureen Keegan (Darden, '15)
25. Colin Keeler (Wharton, '19)
26. Ryan Lee (Johnson, '19)
27. Mark Larik (Anderson, '19)
28. Charlie Mangiardi (NYU Stern, '17)
29. Ravi Maniar (UNC Kenan-Flagler, '16)
30. Anne McKenna (Darden, '19)
31. Adam Miller (Darden, '20)
32. Emily Moore (Anderson, '20)
33. Tony Morash (UNC Kenan-Flagler, '16)
34. Iman Nanji (Anderson, '20)
35. Jordan Nichols (Ross, '14)
36. Prawee Nonthapun (Kellogg, '19)
37. Richard Porter (UNC Kenan-Flagler, '16)
38. Taylor O'Brien (McCombs, '17)
39. Jason Perocho (UNC Kenan-Flagler, '15)
40. Bryce Parrish (UNC Kenan-Flagler, '16)
41. David Rokeach (Fuqua, '15)
42. Andrés Romero (McDonough, '19)
43. Loretta Richardson (McDonough, '20)
44. Sarah Rumbaugh (Darden, '15)
45. Ariadne Sabatoski (Fuqua, '19)
46. Julio Santil (Haas, '14)
47. Ruchi Singh (Foster, '20)
48. Marshelle Slayton (Foster, '19)
49. Bryan Smith (Foster, '20)
50. Kirsten Smith (UNC Kenan-Flagler, '20)
51. Rob Stein, (Kellogg, '17)
52. Stephanie Simpson (Ross, '21)
53. Melanee Swanson (UNC Kenan-Flagler, '17)
54. Ben Thayer (UNC Kenan-Flagler, '16
55. Grace Tong (Fuqua, '19)
56. Nathan Turner (Marriott, '15)
57. Anna Ward (NYU Stern, '20)
58. Ashley Wells (Wharton, '16)

Resources

If you are considering an MBA degree, or currently in business school, there are lots of resources available in addition to this book that can help you navigate your time in business school. Here are a few of my personal favorites.

BeenThere

BeenThere is an online advice marketplace focused on and around MBA talent. Our 150+ mentors from top MBA programs help individuals achieve their career goals through tailored application and career assistance. https://beenthere.mba/

RelishCareers

The goal at Relish is to help job candidates and employers streamline their recruiting processes and make more informed hiring and career decisions. https://www.relishcareers.com/

The Consortium for Graduate Study in Management

The Consortium for Graduate Study in Management is a continually growing and evolving alliance of some of the world's leading graduate business schools and business organizations, supported by the strength of our extended network of students and alumni. The Consortium awards merit-based, full-tuition fellowships to top MBA candidates who have a proven record of promoting inclusion in school, in their jobs or in their personal lives. https://cgsm.org/

Reaching Out MBA (ROMBA)

Reaching Out MBA (ROMBA) has become a year-round operating nonprofit organization with over a dozen unique programs dedicated to educating, inspiring, and connecting the LGBTQ MBA community to impact change in the workplace and create the next generation of leaders. https://www.reachingoutmba.org/

Forté

Forté has provided access to education, opportunities, and a supportive network to empower women in business education and management leadership since 2001. Forté is committed to "changing the balance of power in the workplace" and strives to provide women with the resources they need to advance their careers and become leaders in business. Forté has several programs and events for women who are considering an MBA. Forté MBA Forums are free events held in nine U.S. cities, Toronto, and London, where admissions reps, alumnae, and students from top business schools share insights on the value of an MBA.

Forté MBALaunch is a 10-month program that provides women planning to apply to business school with a roadmap through the application process. It includes intensive GMAT prep, a peer support network, in-person and virtual events, interview practice, and more. The program is held in 11 cities, and they also offer a virtual version. Upon completion, participants receive application fee waivers to more than Forté partner schools.

Forté MBA Fellowships are available to women pursuing a full-time, part-time or executive MBA education at Forté sponsor business schools. To date, the schools have awarded $180 million in Forté Fellowships, helping nearly 8,000 women earn and pursue an MBA.

Forté also holds two conferences for MBA students each year. The Forté MBA Women's Leadership conference is a two-day conference where women can explore career paths, hear from influential businesswomen, and network with recruiters, mentors, and peers. Forté Financial Services FAST Track is a free one-and-a-half day conference focused

on finance careers. It's an opportunity to connect with top financial firms and learn what it's like to work in finance from women leaders in the field.
http://www.fortefoundation.org

Management Leadership for Tomorrow

Launched in 2002, Management Leadership for Tomorrow (MLT) is a national nonprofit organization that is transforming the career and life trajectories of a new generation of diverse leaders. MLT is also expanding its partners' talent pipelines at more than 150 leading corporations, social enterprises, and universities. MLT's acclaimed programs propel the careers of high-potential African American, Latino, and Native American women and men—more than 7,000 and growing. MLT Provides MBA Prep Programs to African American, Latino, and Native American professionals interested in exploring business school. These programs offer personalized guidance to navigate the business school application process as well as the MBA experience itself. MLT participants get access to:

- Personalized coaching to develop a winning game plan for admission;
- Access to top MBA program admissions officers at three seminars that are hosted by our business school and corporate partners;
- Deep experience and knowledge to cultivate personal clarity and help fellows identify which schools are the best fit;
- A network of high-performing peers in the MLT community.

Post MBA Insider: Bonus Resources

Ways to Continue your Learning

- **Feedback -** Questions, success stories or feedback to share? Send me a note - al@mbaschooled.com or share your story with the hashtag #MBAInsider
- **Bonus Resources -** Access additional resources such as toolkits, checklists and podcasts about how to make the most of your MBA Experience. You can find this by signing up for them at www.mbaschooled.com/mba-insider-bonus or by emailing al@mbaschooled.com
- **MBA Content -** For ongoing blogposts on business school, check out www.mbaschooled.com

I hope *MBA Insider* has proven to be a helpful guide on your journey. Visit my blogs and connect with me on social media at:

www.mbaschooled.com

www.careerschooled.com

Twitter: @Alex_Dea

I invite you to take a moment and leave your review on Amazon. Thank you!

INDEX

Printed in Great Britain
by Amazon

39502189R00161